Anna Brooker taught at primary level, [...] with special needs, for nearly twenty ye[ars ...] profession to write, and work with famili[es ...] co-ordinating parenting courses, baptism [...] in' and teaching groups for under-fives. [...] *Cambridge, she is now ordained in the Church of England, working in a parish in West London. Anna is married to Nick, and they have two daughters and one son, all teenagers.*

Text copyright © Anna Brooker 2004
The author asserts the moral right
to be identified as the author of this work

Published by
The Bible Reading Fellowship
First Floor, Elsfield Hall
15–17 Elsfield Way, Oxford OX2 8FG

ISBN 1 84101 260 2
First published 2004
10 9 8 7 6 5 4 3 2 1 0
All rights reserved

Acknowledgments
Scripture quotations are taken from the Contemporary English Version of the Bible published by HarperCollins Publishers, copyright © 1991, 1992, 1995 American Bible Society.

p. 44: 'Having our tea' from *Bobi Jones: Selected Poems*, 1987 (translated from the Welsh by Joseph Clancey), used with permission of Dinefwr Press & Publishers
p. 84: 'Lord, what can you make of me?' by Emily Drew, Danetree School, West Ewell, Surrey. First published in *Our poems and no messin'*, Scripture Union, 1999, used by permission
p. 123: 'A wish for my children' by Evangeline Paterson, from *Lucifer, with Angels*, 1993, used with permission of Dedalus Press, Dublin
p. 142: 'A Celtic blessing for those whom we love' by George McLean, from *Praying with Celtic Christians*, 1988, used with permission of SPCK

A catalogue record for this book is available from the British Library

Printed and bound in Great Britain by
Bookmarque, Croydon

WHY SIBLINGS MATTER

Growing strong relationships in church and community

ANNA BROOKER

For my sister Mair and my brother John, and all my brothers- and sisters-in-law: not only relations, but good friends.

And for Nick, Fiona, Alice and Joe, who keep me 'a fan of families'.

ACKNOWLEDGMENTS

I am grateful to all the friends and relatives who have shared their experiences of siblings, and allowed me to quote them.

Special thanks to Penny Phillips, who first encouraged me to write, and to my editor, Sue Doggett, for all her help and encouragement along the way.

CONTENTS

Foreword 6

Introduction: Parable in the park 7

1 Under the umbrella 12
   Foundations for the family

2 Branching out 29
   Preparing for and adjusting to parenthood

3 Second helpings 46
   The new dynamics of sibling relationships

4 When the bough breaks 65
   Sibling rivalry, fairness and forgiveness

5 Roots and shoots 84
   The family as a nurturing community

6 Out on a limb 104
   Enabling children to develop their identity and independence

7 New horizons 125
   Adolescence and teenagers, human maturity and relationships

8 Siblings matter 144
   The challenge to the church to be community; growing through mutual dependence and trust

Epilogue: Return to the park 165

Further reading 168

Books for children 170

Subject index 172

Bible index 174

FOREWORD

It is a privilege to commend Anna's work, especially as we share a God-given burden about family life. This book offers insights grounded in personal experience as well as rooted in helpful scriptural background.

On this rare and important subject of 'why siblings matter', Anna holds together a breadth and depth of insight and reflection about family life, contributing pertinent, relevant, insightful wisdom and understanding from a broad base of personal experience. She offers creative and practical ideas concerning the necessary building blocks for healthy family relationships from babyhood to adolescence.

With vulnerable honesty Anna explores the delicate 'balancing act' of family life. She walks us through the joys and responsibilities of parenthood and challenges us to support families and contribute to building children's self esteem and confidence. She views human frailties in relationships from a godly perspective and spiritual hope, exploring their complexities, surprises, challenges and pain. She urges us towards the goal of both the family and the church becoming 'dynamic, nurturing communities'.

I have two enduring images from this book: first, the need for elasticity in family relationships, particularly in adolescence; and second, the image of the black walnut tree that opens and closes the book—a poignant reminder that branches break off due to 'heartwood' decay, the tree no longer supple enough to withstand the storms. I hope and pray that this book will inspire and challenge you to build strong relationships and that your 'heartwood' will grow supple and strong in Christ, able to withstand the winds of transition and change in all your family relationships.

Jackie Cray
Formerly Advisor for Families and Under Fives, Church Pastoral Aid Society (CPAS)

INTRODUCTION

PARABLE IN THE PARK

The Lord said: I will bless those who trust me. They will be like trees growing beside a stream—trees with roots that reach down to the water, and with leaves that are always green.
JEREMIAH 17:7–8

Storm-force winds and heavy flooding in the autumn of 2000 led to great distress for many people who saw their homes and possessions damaged and destroyed. In the area of west London where I live, we were mercifully spared this, thanks to the efficacy of the Thames Barrier, controlling the volume of water in the river downstream. Nevertheless, the Thames was fuller than I have ever seen it and its force and destructive potential were plain for all to see. The waters covered the towpath between Richmond and Twickenham, and the riverside picnic sites and playing fields at Marble Hill Park were flooded. These same fields had witnessed in the preceding weeks a heady mix of rugby matches, school sports days, sunbathers, daily dog-walkers and summer concert-goers enjoying champagne evenings.

Amid the rising waters, one tree stood secure as others gave way. It was the ancient black walnut, which stands in its own enclosure by the gate to the riverside. Stretching outwards as far as it stretches upwards, it is a landmark in the park, particularly when the ground it canopies becomes carpeted in purple crocuses every spring. Some of its broadest boughs are propped and held from above to strengthen them under the weight of higher branches, and though it looks blackened and lifeless in winter, each spring proves its vigour as new leaves appear. Who can guess how far its roots extend? What is certain is that it has a constant source of water from the neighbouring River Thames.

A parable for our times? For many people today, life can feel as fickle as the scene I have just described. One day, green fields filled with happy faces; the next, all security washed away as unresolved tensions, hurts and differences, added to the everyday pressures of family life, overwhelm them. What is there to cling on to at such times? Friends, relatives, colleagues, the church?

The gospel offers hope, forgiveness and a fresh start to those who suffer family breakdown, who have been uprooted or dispossessed by it. Many have written expertly and very helpfully on this theme, and it is not the remit of this book. Rather, we shall look at how family relationships can *grow strong* to withstand the external and internal pressures of today's world, and at the biblical principles that may be applied to practical issues common to all relationships.

In particular, we will consider how the *horizontal* relationships within families, especially those of siblings, can strengthen the whole unit as much as do the *vertical*, parent–child relationships which have been the focus of so much attention in recent years. Most parents would like their children to have at least one sibling as a friend, playmate and ally throughout life, outlasting the parent–child bonds. While researching this book, I questioned many adults of all ages about their experiences of sibling relationships. Two common threads connected all their responses—that they cared very deeply about their own brothers and sisters, and that they wanted their children to have strong relationships with each other. One person commented: 'This has made me appreciate a lot more of how important these relationships are for future relationships and attitudes.'

Another told me how her mother's greatest regret in life, despite having a large and happy family of her own, was that she had never got on with her only sibling. The sense of loss of friendship with an older brother was, and is, acute, and her relationship with him remains distant.

A father of four, who was an only child himself, expressed how upset he felt when his children hurt each other, because he would have loved to have had a sibling. Others, now enjoying being grandparents, expressed it like this: 'Whatever we did or didn't do (as parents)—the greatest and most overwhelming satisfaction and happiness is given to us by the boys' current good relationships, and indeed between their wives.'

I concluded that sibling relationships are of fundamental importance to people of all ages, though older people tend to be more aware of that importance. Yet, despite the widespread recognition of it, very little attention is paid to siblings in books and articles about parenting and families. As I read widely on these themes, I was struck repeatedly by the way sibling relationships are overlooked. For example, the illuminating report, *Something to Celebrate* (NS/CHP, 1995), talks about the power of forgiveness in the family, and its impact on society:

How does the work of salvation express itself in relation to the family? ... It happens when husband and wife or a parent and child learn to forgive one another ... It happens when barriers of hostility or indifference separating one generation from another or one family from another are broken down and people find a unity in love.[1]

Here, as so often, the importance of the couple's relationship, and of those between parents and children, is highlighted, but those between siblings are overlooked. Yet experience tells us that how siblings relate is a major factor in the health not just of the nuclear family, but also of the wider family community. As if to reinforce this truth, many of the major stories of family breakdown and reconciliation in the Bible feature siblings at their heart, from Cain and Abel to Jacob and Esau, to Joseph and his brothers. I hope that the following pages will go some way to redress the balance in writing about families.

Like the family trees beloved of Old Testament writers, the black walnut tree in Marble Hill Park has grown horizontally as well as vertically in its many decades of life; it is comfortably as broad as it is high. So we will look at how the 'wider family' in human terms can grow strong enough to support many who might otherwise be lonely and vulnerable. Also we will consider how the 'family' of the local church can and should be growing strong in the love and acceptance it provides, first for its members and then for those who seek shelter under its umbrella.

✣

This book follows the stages of family life and sibling relationships, starting with the parents' relationship and the birth of their first child, before focusing on siblings and the dynamics of the family. This progression is echoed in the 'Bible focus' sections, which conclude each chapter and look at biblical examples of relationships and the principles that they demonstrate.

Each chapter ends with a summary, 'In a nutshell', and a number of 'Growth points' which suggest ways of thinking further about the issues raised.

These are followed by 'Clearings', which offer the opportunity to consider the topic from another angle, through poetry and scripture. Try to allow up to twenty minutes for this further reading and reflection. A prayer is also provided. I hope that these times will lead us into the discoveries that C.S. Lewis described as 'patches of God-light in the woods of our experience'.[2]

The book is designed to be read by individuals and groups. If you are reading it alone, you may find it most helpful to read a chapter at a time—for example, daily or weekly—and to allow time for your ideas to develop before moving on. Do make notes as you go along, and look back on them once you finish the book.

Groups could use the book as the basis for a parenting course, home group, cell group or informal discussion group. The chapters are self-contained, providing material for eight sessions. If possible, each group member should read the main body of the chapter in advance, and come prepared to discuss the 'Growth points'. Some groups may wish to consider the 'Bible focus' material together, rather than reading it in advance.

The subject of relationships is one that affects people negatively as well as positively.

Much that is discussed in groups will be personal and sensitive. A simple group agreement can be helpful in establishing trust and support—for example, 'Play your part; Give others a chance; Respect confidences'.

'Clearings' could be used as a reflective conclusion to each meeting. If the pieces are to be read aloud, ask someone to prepare this in advance, and consider playing quiet music in the background.

NOTES

1 *Something to Celebrate*, NS/CHP, 1995, p. 92
2 C.S. Lewis, *Letters to Malcolm: Chiefly on Prayer*, Geoffrey Bles, 1964

CHAPTER 1

UNDER THE UMBRELLA: FOUNDATIONS FOR THE FAMILY

Love is a temporary madness, it erupts like volcanoes and then subsides. And when it subsides you have to make a decision. You have to work out whether your roots have so entwined together that it is inconceivable that you should ever part. Because this is what love is... Your mother and I had it, we had roots that grew toward each other underground, and when all the pretty blossom had fallen from our branches we found that we were one tree and not two.[1]

OAKS FROM ACORNS...

It's hard to imagine that the black walnut tree in Marble Hill Park started life as a single nut. Yet the reason we now know its precise age is that the sapling appears in the original design for the landscaped gardens of Marble Hill House in the 1720s. Families, too, have to start somewhere, namely with a relationship between two people, in marriage or cohabitation. At this stage the 'family tree' is very much a sapling, putting down roots and getting established in its own position.

Our garden is littered with fledgling horse chestnut trees. They arrived there courtesy of the local squirrels, which bury them and forget to dig them up; and of our children, who every autumn at primary school collected bags of conkers by the thousand, then distributed them around the garden with their friends, leaving them in the most unlikely places. These saplings remind me of toddlers:

they seem to barge their way in, pushing to the front, absorbing all the nourishment and attention they can get—irritating at times, but you have to admire their enthusiasm. We should really pull up this potential forest, for conkers never take root in the right places; in fact, they usually burst forth immediately next to a particularly delicate plant. I do love to watch them grow, however, launching themselves upwards and strengthening the central trunk as they do so. There are very few lateral branches to start with, just an upward momentum as they seem to grow before our very eyes.

So too with the family unit: the enthusiasm and intensity that enable a couple to put down roots and establish themselves as a unit also strengthen the trunk, which is their relationship as a couple before they 'branch out' into the adventure of parenthood. Indeed, the strength of the relationship between mother and father is known to be a critical factor in their child's development. Psychologists recognize that for a child to be mature, and therefore happy much of the time, he or she needs parents who basically like, respect and trust each other.[2]

The partnership at the centre of a family is the factor that will most influence the well-being of all the family, not just the couple themselves. The best thing a father can do for his children, we are often told, is to love their mother. The same is true, of course, the other way round. In this chapter we will consider the skills and habits that can help to establish the partnership. Although the vast majority of couples now choose to live together for some time before marriage, many also choose to marry before they have children. The Church has been slow to respond to this sea change in social attitudes, and Christians have too often been judgmental and disapproving, rather than actively promoting marriage as the God-given pattern for committed relationships. At whatever stage in their relationship a couple marry, it is a significant step, and one to be supported and celebrated by their friends and family.

All this may sound rather idealistic and naïve, given the frequency of divorce and the number of one-parent families, stepfamilies and those where the parents no longer live together. My purpose at the outset of this book is not to ignore or judge these parents and families, but to consider the importance of the partnership between parents. In the sad event that the couple's relationship breaks down, the skills and habits discussed here, particularly in communication, will be vital both to the adults and their children.

Leaving and cleaving

The sense of a couple becoming a new entity, a new creation of God, is enshrined in the famous verse from Genesis which is in the wedding service: 'For this reason a man will leave his father and mother and be united to his wife, and they will become one flesh' (Genesis 2:24).

We will look now at what the 'leaving and cleaving' (as older versions of the Bible put it) involves. The first is largely dependent on other people; the second on the couple themselves.

For those who get married, the ceremony enables the public recognition and affirmation, by family and friends, of the new family that is being established. Modern wedding services now include this aspect more explicitly, as the minister asks the congregation to support and uphold them, now and in the future. Implicit in this is the sense of 'giving away', which was usually the role of the bride's father in years gone by. The couple need to be allowed to leave their previous family, whether a home with parents or one with friends, in order to commit themselves to each other. Whether a couple marry or not, the 'leaving' aspect is crucial, for it is only then that the new entity can begin to take shape and two individuals be brought together in a lasting and committed partnership.

Members of the wider family can facilitate this 'leaving' process by relating to the couple together—for example, by parents talking to their child's partner on the phone rather than insisting that they discuss things only with their son or daughter. Brothers and sisters on both sides can help by accepting and including the new partner. Even a gesture as simple as remembering his or her birthday, and not just that of their brother or sister, can help a great deal. It requires give and take, a readiness to accept different ways of doing things, and an appreciation of the strengths of the new family that is being established. Sometimes it will be very painful for the original families on both sides to accept that the couple are committed now to putting each other first, before parents or siblings. Being willing to release someone in this way very often brings a greater closeness in the long term, however.

Sticking together

So what about the 'cleaving'? This old-fashioned word is defined as meaning 'to adhere or stick to; to join oneself with, to stand by closely and loyally'. Cleaving does not simply mean an intellectual assent or a written contract of partnership, but a whole lifestyle. Each partner pledges to live out their loyalty and commitment to the other. To paraphrase the old saying, the proof of the cleaving is in the living. Loyalty and commitment are perhaps the least fashionable virtues in our society, for they 'cramp our style'—our so-called 'rights' to say and do whatever we want. Loyalty and commitment are, however, fundamental in building relationships of any kind, and supremely so when the couple have children. Only when these foundations are in place can trust develop between the couple. Without trust, any relationship is doomed to fail, so it is vital that loyalty and commitment are not only talked about but demonstrated.

Firm foundations

Trust takes time to build because it involves an element of risk, of stepping outside the boundaries of our own knowledge and control. We need to have confidence in the person we are trusting, and our experience will dictate whether we can do this or not. Trust is simply another word for faith, which needs to be active and specific, rather than passive and general. The Bible tells us, 'Faith makes us *sure* of what we hope for and gives us *proof* of what we cannot see' (Hebrews 11:1, my italics). For a couple, it is each partner's loyalty and commitment to the other which is the *surety* and *proof* of the growing trust between them.

Blondin, the great French showman who crossed Niagara Falls on a tightrope, once did so pushing a wheelbarrow. The crowd roared and cheered. 'We knew you could do it, Blondin!' they yelled. 'We have faith in you!' Bowing to their applause, Blondin motioned to the wheelbarrow. 'Now,' he asked, 'who would like to sit in it this time?' We all know that actions speak louder than words and, in the area of trust in relationships, this is overwhelmingly true. When put to the test, in action, faith either shines more brightly or it is shown to be a hollow shell.

How's your building?

Jesus would have appreciated Blondin's challenge to the crowd. He frequently threw out verbal challenges to his audiences. Sometimes they were accompanied by stories, as when he talked about the two builders (Luke 6:46–49). 'Why do you keep on saying that I am your Lord', Jesus asks the crowd, 'when you refuse to do what I say?' Then he paints a verbal picture of the wise and the foolish men, building houses on rock and sand respectively. The wise man takes much longer to build his house, because digging foundations is hard, slow work. Outwardly and initially, the other builder is much more successful because he finishes the job and moves in while the wise man is still digging.

A contemporary story indeed. As I write this, the city of Jerusalem is in mourning for the many lives lost when a building in the city centre collapsed during a wedding party. The cause? It was built too fast, with inadequate foundations and cheap materials. Then, a number of crucial supporting pillars were removed to make more space for a dance floor, ignoring warnings. Sadly, and sometimes tragically, our children are growing up in a world that values speed above quality, and has forgotten how to wait. How easily we carry over this impatience into our relationships.

Relationship building

When he told his 'house on the rock' story, Jesus was of course talking not about buildings but about people and relationships. If you want to follow me, to be my friend, he tells us, you must take time both to hear and apply what I say in your life. Building a relationship is rather like building a house. As we have already seen, the foundations of loyalty, commitment and trust form the rock on which the house is built. Getting down to the rock involves a lot of clearing and digging, effort and determination.

When we had a small extension built on the back of our house, it took the two builders three days to dig the foundations, by hand. They didn't know in advance how deep they would have to dig, and we were amazed at the mountain of soil removed before they reached the firm base they needed. They spent the next three days pouring in concrete, waiting for it to set, then laying the first rows of bricks to form a sturdy base. That was the first week of building, but there was little to show for it, other than a skip full of rubble. In the second week they really built. Day by day the walls rose; in fact, by the third day, the shell of the building was finished. Magnificent! But building the walls, the part everyone could see, was the easy bit. The hardest work was under the surface.

Habits of a lifetime?

The foundations determine the final shape of the building, as well as its strength. Once the foundations of our extension were dug, we couldn't have strolled up to the builders and asked them to move it to the right a bit, or make it slightly smaller. So too, in a partnership, the habits and patterns of behaviour towards each other determine the 'shape' of the relationship. Although change is never impossible, by the grace of God, it is very difficult to undo foundations laid in the wrong shape or dimensions. How important, then, to take care and time, to weigh up our priorities, such as our use of time and money, just as builders work from plans drawn up with care and accuracy.

Church leaders may need to resist the temptation to persuade a bright young couple to join committees and lead as many groups as possible, either separately or together. However well-matched and 'spiritual' they are, it is certain that the early years together will present them both with unexpected challenges and demands. They will need support and understanding, not extra pressures. The greatest enemy of close and deep relationships is lack of time together, and the church can simply add to the problem.

For better, for worse…

It is one thing to agree to 'love, comfort, honour and protect' each other, as the marriage service puts it, but quite another to stand by your partner when they lose their job, to forgive them when they hurt you, or to refrain from saying 'I told you so' when they make costly mistakes. At a wedding, the words 'for better, for worse; for richer, for poorer; in sickness and in health' rarely seem particularly relevant. It is certain, however, that some or all of them will be tested in the years afterwards, and usually in ways we cannot foresee. You don't know how deep you'll have to go until you start digging, as our builders told us.

Relationships are not easy; they are very hard work. The things that first attracted us to our partner may become those that irritate us most, particularly if we live with someone very different from ourselves. That's why good habits, such as respect, understanding and kindness, are very important. They are the mortar that holds the blocks together under pressure and enable us always to give the other person the benefit of the doubt, to see their point of view, to withhold judgment.

Along the way, there will be many times when it would be easier to give up on the relationship. Couples need good preparation and support, whether from the local church or from relatives or friends. There are so many myths to dispel—the myth of complete personal and sexual fulfilment with a perfect partner, the myth of total agreement about everything, the myth of material comfort in a designer home with a designer partner bringing true happiness... There is a desperate need for us all to promote lifelong partnerships, rather than relationships where all of both partners' personal needs can and should be met, in record time, of course! The marriage vows emphasize this: 'All that I am I give to you, and all that I have I share with you.'[3] But it is all too easy for this contract to be reinterpreted as 'All that you are I demand of you, and all that I have I retain the right to keep.'

Don't get tied down...

Sadly, the way marriage is portrayed in the media today only underlines the second version of the contract. Newly-weds in TV soaps seem unable to make it through their honeymoon before having serious regrets about their marriage; they discuss each other behind their backs with their friends and do each other down in public. After the excitement of the wedding day, hen and stag nights, and presents, it is downhill all the way—hardly a good advertisement for married life, and certainly no incentive to viewers to follow them down the aisle.

There is also a widespread fear of commitment in our culture, produced at least in part by the greater range of choices that we have in every part of our lives. Of course, there have long been jokes about men reluctant to 'tie the knot' or 'get tied down', but in previous generations most people expected to marry and live with the same person for the rest of their lives. I do not believe that this is any longer the case. Indeed, it seems like an impossible dream for many, given the evidence they are likely to have seen of marriage and family breakdown. Surprisingly, and encouragingly, 82 per cent of 16- and 17-year-olds in a recent survey said that they expected to marry, and there is much that can be done to help these marriages to last, but it will be done against a background of pessimism and cynicism. For these days, long marriages are celebrated as rarities, and the participants viewed as saints for staying together so long. A number of Christian organizations are seeking to address this issue, with programmes to educate young people about the importance and benefits of marriage. Charlie Colchester, Executive Director of CARE, comments: 'I believe that marriage is one of the most important social issues facing our generation. Ultimately, the stability of future generations depends on strong families—and strong families depend on strong marriages.'[4]

I read recently of a comprehensive school which enlisted the help of the local church in teaching pupils about the significance of marriage. They staged a 'mock wedding' in church, through which the words of the service and vows were discussed. Recent reports from the United States also indicate a growing awareness of the importance of marriage. In Oklahoma, the state is looking to the voluntary sector, and especially churches, to promote marriage, educate young people and prepare couples thoroughly for what they are undertaking. The state has even persuaded clergy of all denominations to agree not to marry couples unless they wait for four months, during which time they go through a training programme. However unfashionable it may have become, marriage remains 'the best protection against abuse, poverty and disease for every sector of society'.[5]

Make or break

Once they were finished, the wise and foolish men's houses in Jesus' story probably looked quite similar. It was only when the weather changed and a storm arose that the difference between them was revealed. Couples often look back on tough times as those when their relationship grew most, because they saw the evidence of each other's commitment and loyalty at those testing times. Sadly, the opposite may be equally true, and one or both partners may be left crying out, 'Where were you when I needed you?'

This is the case for many couples who have suffered tragic accidents—for example, to one of their children—and whose own relationship has then broken down. The extra stress placed upon them has simply been too great. All the relationships within a family are interdependent, so it is inevitable that when one suffers, all the others will too. It is vital, however, that the partners at the centre of the family receive extra support at these times, because it is very difficult (some would say impossible) to provide support for each other while both are suffering loss or trauma at the same time. This is a crucial time for family, friends and the church to act upon their commitment to support the couple in keeping their relationship strong.

Still strong

Recently I was with a friend who was taken to hospital late at night, while staying away from home. There had been some doubt as to whether she should have gone away at all, due to treatment she was receiving at the time, and so she felt that the emergency was to some extent her fault. As we phoned her husband and asked him to meet us at the hospital, her only concern was for him, his anxiety and his safety. 'Tell him I love him,' she whispered through her pain. When he arrived several hours later, I was waiting outside the ward for news of my friend. He greeted me and went straight in, his only concern to be with her and comfort her. From the moment he arrived, she told me later, she knew that she'd be all right. I had known this couple for years, watched their children grow up and observed them in many of the ups and downs of family life, but that night I was struck afresh by their total commitment and loyalty to each other, the strength of the bond between them in the crisis, and the firm foundations of their family. There were no recriminations or blame; rather, mutual support and comfort, born out of love and trust.

✣

BIBLE FOCUS: TAKEN ON TRUST

Asked what they thought were the implications of a decision to marry, 62 per cent Europe-wide, but 79 per cent in the UK, said it was 'to commit yourself to being faithful to your partner'.[6]

Faith and commitment are very closely linked. Faith, the ability to trust, inspires and enables commitment because it dispels fear and engenders hope. Conversely, it is fear—of missing out, of making a mistake, of being thought less of—that is the greatest obstacle to commitment. Let us see how this applies to couples by looking at the contrasting relationships of Adam and Eve and Mary and Joseph.

The account of Adam and Eve's relationship, in Genesis 2:15—3:24, is short and specific. We learn that Eve was made to be 'a suitable partner' for Adam and that they enjoyed freedom and happiness in the garden of Eden, and a lack of guilt and shame. All of this was lost to Adam and Eve when they succumbed to the serpent's temptation. What a price to pay for one mistake, we may feel, but the error is so fundamental that its consequences are inevitable and far-reaching.

Adam and Eve have a crisis of faith. Eve is unable to accept the minor frustration of not being allowed to eat one fruit of the many—hundreds, perhaps—on offer, nor to trust that God has her and Adam's welfare at heart, so she is open to suggestion from the serpent. She and Adam do not trust God enough to withstand its teasing ('Did God really say…?') or its attempt to cast doubt on God's truthfulness ('You won't really die…').

Once the breakdown of faith in their divine parent has occurred, the breakdown of trust with each other follows swiftly. No doubt Eve resented Adam for not stopping her, as much as Adam resented Eve for taking the forbidden fruit. As we read on, we see how Adam and Eve lose their self-esteem, their sense of identity and security, and hide in the bushes to avoid God, rather as a guilty child runs and hides from a parent when a misdemeanour is discovered. Thus the 'family' relationship with God is lost and they are banished from the garden.

Adam and Eve hide not only their nakedness but also their emotions as they make excuses to God for their actions; they can no longer communicate honestly with each other or with their creator. As the old joke goes, 'Adam blamed Eve, Eve blamed the serpent, and the serpent didn't have a leg to stand on!' Rather than supporting each other, honestly admitting the fault and sharing responsibility for it, they deflect the blame and turn on each other. How this rings true in our own experience, where the tendency to deflect blame on to others is so strong, whether in marriage, sibling relationships or in friendships. 'He did it first'; 'She told me to'; 'They were doing it too'.

We have seen how the first couple's relationship was fatally damaged by lack of trust, first in God and then in each other, and how this led to mutual blaming, deception and anger rather than mutual loyalty, respect and responsibility. It all hinged on faith and Eve's choice not to take God at his word, not to take things on trust: she had to take a bite of the fruit to see if he was telling the truth.

Mary's faith

The contrast with Jesus' mother could hardly be greater. Visited by an angel, out of the blue as it were, Mary's entire life, future hopes and dreams are thrown into turmoil by his message. Yet, by the end of the dialogue with Gabriel, she is able to say, 'I am the Lord's servant! Let it happen as you have said' (Luke 1:38). Mary takes the most gigantic step of faith in entrusting her life into God's hands, for him to use as he chooses. She chooses to believe God, to act upon the faith and love for God that have already found favour in his sight. Her next step is also taken in faith—going off to visit her cousin Elizabeth and to be there for her during her unusual and unexpected pregnancy.

As so often happens when someone acts in kindness and generosity to another, the benefit is two-way, for, through Elizabeth, God provides affirmation of the promise he has made to Mary. The significance of Mary's pregnancy, which can scarcely yet have been certain in physical terms, is revealed to Elizabeth, who greets her young cousin as 'the mother of my Lord'. Elizabeth recognizes Mary's faith: 'The Lord has blessed you because you believed that he will keep his promise' (Luke 1:43, 45).

It takes two

While Luke tells us Mary's story in the opening chapters of his Gospel, Matthew is concerned with Joseph's part, beginning the story with the genealogies that place Joseph firmly in the family line descended from King David. To his original readers, the early Jewish Christians, this was crucial in showing how Jesus' birth fulfilled all the Old Testament promises concerning the Messiah. But what does Matthew tell us about Joseph himself, apart from his family tree?

He is first described as 'a righteous man' and, because of this, he initially decides quietly to break off his engagement to Mary in order to save her public disgrace. He takes time to consider this, however, and so is open to hear God's advice on the matter. Like his Old Testament namesake, Joseph is a dreamer, and God sends an angel at night to tell him what is really going on. At this point, Joseph too has a choice to make. Should he follow common sense and divorce Mary anyway, since no one would blame him for protecting both himself and her from shame and disgrace? Or could he possibly believe what God has told him—the humanly impossible, unbelievably wonderful news that the long-awaited Messiah is soon to be born to his fiancée?

Matthew does not record Joseph's struggle, only his decision: 'After Joseph woke up, he and Mary were soon married, just as the Lord's angel had told him to do. But they did not sleep together before her baby was born. Then Joseph named him Jesus' (Matthew 1:24–25).

At this point, Joseph takes on the full responsibility for being Mary's husband and Jesus' human father. He also lays aside any right to protest, now or in the future, that the child is not his. Instead, he accepts the role God gives him, to protect, nurture, discipline and love Jesus. Indeed, Jesus is recognized as a member of the house of David; he is 'adopted' before he is born and becomes an heir to the royal line through Joseph's faith. Luke traces this line back not just to King David but to Adam, in showing how Jesus is the saviour not only of the Jewish nation but of all humankind.

Joseph continues to act in faith as he takes care of his wife and young family in the months following his marriage to Mary. First there is the unexpected trek to Bethlehem for the census, later the hurried escape to Egypt to avoid Herod's massacre and their subsequent return to Nazareth. At each stage, Joseph hears and obeys God's instructions, often given to him in dreams.

Silent strength

The Gospel writers are silent about the qualities of Mary and Joseph's relationship. We can only assume that the hardships they faced together would have increased their love, respect and trust for each other. The honesty that, of necessity, characterized their early days together must have helped to lay firm foundations. Indeed, unconventional as it was, pressurized as the early years must have been, we may surmise that they had a happy home, for Jesus 'became wise, and he grew strong. God was pleased with him and so were the people' (Luke 2:52).

We know that they had more children after Jesus, for Jesus had brothers and sisters. Indeed, his brother James is thought to have been a leader in the early Church. The strongest bond between them, however, was their faith in God and in his loving purposes for their lives. We know that Mary was not an overly controlling parent; she treasured things in her heart, seeking answers in prayer, rather than restricting Jesus' development, because she could not fully understand his divine calling.

Most of all, in considering Mary and Joseph and the family they built, we have the evidence of Jesus' adult life and ministry. We can see the depth of his friendships, his ability to relate to people of all ages, races and backgrounds, his sense of identity and his amazing maturity as a human being. All this leads us to believe that he grew up in a home that was full of love, trust and security—the result in large part of Mary and Joseph's strong relationship.

❖

IN A NUTSHELL

This opening chapter focused on relationships as the foundation for family life. Family, friends and the local church can support couples by releasing them to be a new family in their own right, and can alert them to likely pressures and unrealistic expectations of each other.

For the couple themselves, good habits of loyalty and commitment help to build trust and to ensure that the family's foundations are strong. Jesus' story of the two house builders illustrates this need for solid foundations. In the 'Bible focus' section, the relationships of Adam and Eve and Mary and Joseph were contrasted, to show again the need for trust, both in God and in each other.

GROWTH POINTS

- Consider how attitudes to marriage and cohabitation have changed, especially in the past ten years. What reasons would you give for these changes? How do they affect (a) family and friends of young couples, and (b) the local church?

- How can Christians best promote healthy relationships between couples? What could be done to help couples facing 'make or break' points in their relationships? Think practically and realistically about this.

- For further study, read Matthew 7:24–27. Make a drawing (or, in a group, a poster), showing two houses. Label the ground on which each is built by showing the qualities, positive and negative, that make it 'solid rock' or 'shifting sand'. Now label the pictures to show the 'rain, floods and winds' that can threaten relationships. Once you have completed both drawings, bring the qualities, the pressures and problems to God in prayer, asking for his strength and help to build strong relationships. (You may like to pin up the 'house on the rock' picture, and to crumple up the 'house on the sand' to show its crash in the storm.)

CLEARINGS

Theirs was that substantial affection which arises... when the two who are thrown together begin first by knowing the rougher sides of each other's character, and not the best till further on, the romance growing up in the interstices of a mass of hard prosaic reality...

The compounded feeling proves itself to be the only love which is as strong as death—that love which many waters cannot quench, nor the floods drown, beside which the passion usually called by the name is evanescent as steam.[7]

PRAYER

Pray for yourself and your partner, or for another couple in your community of family and friends.

May their (our) relationship be life-giving and life-long,
enriched by your presence and strengthened by your grace;
may they (we) bring comfort and confidence to each other
in faithfulness and trust.
Lord of life and love:
Hear our prayer.[8]

NOTES

1 *Something to Celebrate*, NS/CHP, 1995, p. 92
2 Strean and Freeman, *Raising Cain*, Oxford: Facts on File, 1988, p. 163
3 'Marriage', *Common Worship*, Pastoral Services, Church House Publishing, 2001, p. 109
4 *Breakthrough* magazine, CARE, Summer 2001
5 Melanie Phillips, 'The bond that binds us', *The Sunday Times*, 24 June 2001
6 *Something to Celebrate*, p. 51
7 Thomas Hardy, *Far from the Madding Crowd*, 1874, chapter 56
8 Adapted from *Common Worship*, Pastoral Services, Marriage, p. 112

CHAPTER 2

BRANCHING OUT: PREPARING FOR AND ADJUSTING TO PARENTHOOD

> *Since you've arrived, days have melted into night and back again and we are learning a new grammar, a big sentence whose punctuation marks are feeding and winding and nappy changing and these occasional moments of quiet... Your coming has turned me upside down and inside out.*[1]

First-time parents have a unique awareness of the precious and miraculous nature of the new life in their care. The whole world now seems to revolve around a baby and the new patterns and priorities it brings. The greatest challenge for parents at this stage is that parent–child relationships now coexist with, and may threaten, the couple's own bond. If the 'family tree' of the parents' relationship is not firmly rooted, the addition of branches at this time will certainly destabilize it and may even threaten to uproot it.

That is only to consider the 'nuclear' family, however. When a couple have children, they also begin or extend their parents' roles as grandparents and their siblings' roles as aunts and uncles, while their nieces and nephews acquire a new cousin, and so on. Two of our favourite photographs of our first child show her being held by her grandmother and by one of her uncles, neither of whom had ever had a grandchild or a niece before and whose faces show the joy and wonder of meeting her.

These wider family relationships are a source of much satisfaction. 'He enjoys being adored by his nephews,' wrote one mother of her bachelor brother, with great affection. Children love this sense of wider family too. My nephew celebrated his tenth birthday two days after our first child was born. He told me that the best thing about the gift we sent that year was the card, which we'd signed 'from Nick, Anna and the baby, if it's arrived by then!' Similarly, we have a photo of our children in the garden, shelling peas, which we always think of as 'Josh's birthday picture'. I left the pea-shelling to answer the phone, and it was my brother-in-law telling us that their first child had arrived safely. I rushed straight out to tell the children, who were every bit as excited as I was, and posed for a celebratory photo.

Before considering the impact of a baby's arrival on the network of relationships involved, let's look back to where it all starts.

Great expectations

A television superhero marries an 'earthling' and, several episodes later, they discover she is pregnant. She wonders why she is putting on weight so fast, only to be told by the superhero that, where he comes from, pregnancy only lasts six days. Bemused by her horrified reaction, he mutters about the ridiculous notion of waiting for nine months to give birth. He is unable to understand the problem, since mothers on his planet merely programme their children to behave how they want them to, following the script of standard instructions which all parents use. Very simple, and light years away from the complexities of being a human parent.

I still remember vividly the afternoon when I walked to the chemist's at the end of our road to buy a pregnancy testing kit. In those days, you had to wait a whole hour for the result, so we had plenty of time to think about what we would do next, depending on whether the vital blue ring appeared. There was such a heady mixture of elation and total shock when the test was positive. We both knew that life would never be the same again, as they say, and that we were embarking on a journey to an unknown destination, along routes we hadn't travelled before. Help!

Something old, something new

One of the greatest challenges of life as a couple is to take on board our partner's personal background, with all its strengths and weaknesses, and recognize that it is significantly different from our own. It may be even harder to allow one's partner to do the same for us. The experiences that we bring with us into a relationship, particularly from our family and childhood, will be highly influential in determining what our own family is like. We seek to celebrate the good and be freed from the not-so-good, to glean the best from both sides as we work out the patterns and values of our own relationship. These patterns and habits will form the foundations of the family into which children are born. We may scarcely be aware of the process going on, until the arrival of our first child. Then, suddenly it all leaps into focus and we realize that the way we were parented is not the only way of doing it; indeed, in our partner's view, it is probably the *wrong* way of doing it, because it is not what they experienced.

It takes time to adjust to seeing one's partner as a parent, but it is also vital to give them support and encouragement in their role. As a new mum, I felt very unsure of myself, but I wish I had recognized earlier that Nick felt just as much a novice as I did. Even with couples where one partner has had children before, there is still a newness and nervousness as the first child of a new partnership is born, and it really helps to acknowledge this together and avoid pretending that we're coping when we're not. Simple things can make a huge difference, such as not undermining each other and not telling each other what to do, particularly in front of other people. If we start off in the wrong way, we are likely still to be doing it when our children are old enough to hear us, resulting in insecurity and confusion for them.

In the early days, we also lay ourselves open to unsolicited advice from parents and others, which can put a real strain on our relationship. Advice can be invaluable, but only when we ask for it and are prepared to act upon it, not when it comes to fill the gap created by parents' failure to back each other up. It's well worth starting as we mean to go on and supporting each other, even when we don't agree with how our partner does things. This is a specific and very valuable fruit of the loyalty that is such a fundamental quality to cultivate in relationships.

Be prepared

As we've already seen, waiting is often thought of negatively, as a waste of time. Fortunately, in the matter of children, we don't have a choice. Parenthood is a lifetime commitment and the months of pregnancy are necessary preparation. While every family is unique, most face the same critical 'key points', and the better prepared for them we are, the more likely our family is to survive. In Chapters 6 and 7 we will look at these in detail, but for now we will focus on the first, and most memorable, 'key point' of all—the arrival of the first child. For this to be met with confidence, the parents need to be relating to each other already as family partners, as well as a romantic couple. Whatever pressures we have faced as a couple before having children, we will experience new and far more challenging ones afterwards. Or, as a friend of mine tells her childless female friends, 'If you can't face your partner without make-up before you are pregnant, you may find morning sickness, breast-feeding and permanent exhaustion quite difficult.'

Once our initial shock and excitement had subsided, and the hormones had kicked in, we soon realized that nine months was not nearly such a long time as we had thought. Alongside the baby's physical development, the household preparations and the financial implications of the pregnancy, there was another crucial process taking place. We were adjusting to the idea of being parents and to seeing each other in that role. It was difficult to imagine what it would be like to be three instead of two, and to be responsible for another human being—their physical, spiritual, emotional and social well-being.

We were fortunate to have friends with young children, and we often discussed families with them and with each other. We were conscious even then that there is no 'right way' to parent, no blueprint for a happy family or a contented baby. It was fascinating to watch couples we knew make the transition into parenthood. In some cases, the woman seemed to take on almost exclusive responsibility for the baby; in others it was much more shared, and in still others, the father was far more tuned in to the baby's needs and development than the mother. What seemed to matter was not who did what, but whether both parents were comfortable with their roles and supportive of each other. For this to happen, good communication is crucial as the couple work out in advance what are their expectations of 'family life'. Being prepared is key: it is very difficult to hold such discussions once we are into the exhausting and demanding early months of parenthood.

Bible blueprint?

For Christians, there is the added dimension of what God wants for their family, and of the principles that the Bible sets out for parents. It can be all too easy for Christian couples to think that they already know what each other thinks because of this, but there is no biblical blueprint for a Christian family, any more than for any other. We have only to look at Abraham and Sarah, Hannah and Samuel, or Ruth, Naomi and Boaz to see that God is far more creative in his approach to family life than we often allow him to be. Honest discussion of the issues, of each parent's expectations, hopes and fears, is as vital for Christians as for everyone else. Being a Christian is no guarantee of a happy family, any more than it is of happy relationships.

Welcome to the world

'Welcome to the world, Fiona Clare' read the greeting on a hand-painted card from close friends. And it really did feel like a global event, momentous and earth-shattering, as if we were the only couple ever to have had a baby, to have shared in the miracle of creation. The friend who painted that card recently became a father for the first time, and we see in him just the same blend of wonder and gratitude that we experienced fifteen years before.

The succeeding days were lived in extremes—of joy and happiness, frustration and despair—as we came to terms with the demands of a new baby. A spell in hospital brought anguish and fear, but also a strengthening of the bonds between us as parents: we needed each other now more than we ever had before. We were especially conscious of the prayers and practical support of our local church family. I vividly remember the visit to us in hospital of one of our ministers, who just appeared one morning, in jeans and a dog-collar, explaining that the collar was a very useful way of being allowed in outside visiting hours. He and his wife had lost their first child in infancy some months earlier, and we were deeply touched by his compassion and prayers for us, as well as being delighted to see an old friend rather than another nurse with a syringe.

Learning to parent

The best advice I was given in those early months came from my health visitor, who told me to follow my instinct because, as Fiona's mother, I was likely to know better than anyone else what she needed. This was so liberating and encouraging, particularly as she followed it through by listening and advising as I made mistakes and falteringly worked out the daily pattern of how I was going to be a mum. Each parent needs to find their own style, and often children benefit greatly from the contrasting approaches of their two parents. Our children would always run to their dad when they fell over as toddlers, which I found hard at times. But they recognized instinctively how compassionate he is and how good at giving hugs when most needed.

Each person's experience of parenthood will be different, and much of this depends on circumstances, particularly those connected with health. Some parents find their lives taken over by doctor's and hospital appointments—or, worse, by weeks in hospital as their former lives and their own needs are swallowed up in caring for a sick baby. For others, the baby's birth is a traumatic experience, resulting in health problems for the mother, frequently exacerbated by post-natal depression, which is more likely to strike in these circumstances. If the pregnancy has been anxious or difficult, this will affect the parents' approach to the baby and their anxiety levels in caring for him or her. Even if there are no such health problems, the needs of the young family will be great as they settle down to life together.

The importance of support for new mothers from the extended family at this time has long been recognized in all cultures:

Every mother-to-be was part of a community of women—family members and neighbours—who shared ideas and helped each other before, during and after each birth. Women worked together to mark each stage of pregnancy with ritual, help to ease a mother's labour and to celebrate a baby's transition to life and the woman's transition to motherhood. In medieval Europe, they were called God-sibs—literally 'sisters in God', and social and economic barriers dissolved as women reached out to help each other.[2]

WWJD (What Would Jesus Do?)

Extended support for young families is crucial, but is no longer as readily available as it once was, due to the fragmentation of family networks, both geographically and relationally. Thus, the local church has an important role to play, not only for its members but in the wider local community. We need to affirm and encourage parents as much as possible, and especially to be on the lookout for those suffering from post-natal depression. It has been found that, while the incidence of such depression is rarely reduced by 'community' support, the recovery rate from it is vastly improved by very simple care, which could be summarized as 'being there'. I long to see local churches acting on this, and 'being there'. This might mean a group or a drop-in for parents, or a visiting team, or 'meals on wheels' for families who've just had a new baby. A friendly word, a listening ear or a quick phone call at regular intervals can make a world of difference to a new mother, teetering on the brink of the downward spiral into post-natal depression. It's what Jesus would do, so let's do it! Parenthood is the most important job we ever do, and the one closest to the heart of God, as Jesus makes very clear:

'Let the children come to me! Don't try to stop them. People who are like these little children belong to the kingdom of God. I promise you that you cannot get into God's kingdom, unless you accept it the way a child does.' Then Jesus took the children in his arms and blessed them by placing his hands on them.
MARK 10:14–16

Parenthood is, however, one of the few jobs for which no training is either provided or, indeed, seen to be required. That's why parenting courses and parents' support groups are gaining popularity. In one local church, an initial course three years ago has multiplied to ten or more groups each year, with 70 per cent of the participants drawn from the local community. In another church, a group of teenage mothers, who first met at the church youth club, now get together in the same hall one afternoon per week, and benefit from the continued friendship and support and the opportunity to meet health visitors and social workers, who provide informal advice and help for the group. In this way the local church is seeking to fill the vacuum left by wider family networks, which exist far less commonly in modern Britain than they did in the past.

Friends like us

Parents have a great deal in common, despite the uniqueness of each person's experience. This is especially true for first-time parents, who can probably offer each other the best support and friendship at this stage. One church ran a group specifically for first-time parents—a drop-in for an afternoon every week, with toys, refreshments, and a leader on hand who was simply there to listen and to hold babies when needed. One of the mothers from the group, reflecting on her first year of parenthood, commented, 'This has been the best year of my life!' It was wonderful to hear, and all the more so because she had waited some years to be a mother. In addition, she had struggled through months of poor sleeping and feeding with a distressed baby, who was finally diagnosed with a severe allergic condition. It certainly wasn't an easy year for her, but the support of others, in a place where she could be honest about how tough it was, helped to ensure that the bond between mother and baby grew strong.

The friendships built up in this church group will continue long after the baby stage, and the children will develop friendships too, which in some cases may last through into school days and beyond. Many parents will count among their closest personal friends those who had children at the same time as them. My mother enjoyed one such friendship for over forty years, right until her death in her 80s. She had first met her friend Margaret at church, and later found herself in the next bed in hospital after they had both had babies. Their friendship carried them through many ups and downs of family life, and their sons became, and remain, good friends. For example, after my father's death, it was Margaret who recognized both Mum's needs and her abilities. She persuaded Mum to join her, working for a local charity—a move that gave Mum much-needed self-esteem, friendship and purpose as she adjusted to widowhood.

What about Dad?

There is no preparation anywhere for fatherhood. How do men get ready for it? Unprepared for what it will mean, men often act in one of two ways. They may decide that their best contribution is to make lots of money and disappear completely into their work. Or the father tries to get far too close, saying things like, 'We are pregnant' and fussing around pretending he is having a baby as well. Finding the right balance is difficult.[3]

Fathers need support just as much as mothers do, for their role as parents is equally crucial. Recent initiatives from Christian organizations such as CARE for the Family and YMCA are beginning to address this need, and much can be done by local churches. Mothers tend to predominate in daytime groups and women are often more ready to admit their needs and discuss them. Perhaps the most effective support for a new dad is to have a friend who is at the same stage, or a little further on, with whom he can share the joys and frustrations over a pint or after a football match. If he has a brother who has a family, this relationship will often be especially helpful at this stage. My husband has three younger brothers, all of whom now have children, and the bonds between them as fathers are stronger as a result. They frequently spend as long on the phone to each other as my sister and I do. Many parents I asked said how much their relationships with siblings had been deepened by the shared experience of parenthood. For example, one mother wrote of her younger sister, who was resented in childhood, 'It's surprising what marriage and children do in bringing people closer together—similar circumstances and all that!'

Gratitude and gift

We have already touched on the miracle of new life, the sense of life as a gift, which is quite overwhelming for almost all parents. It is the starting point for faith for many who have either known and lost, or never known, the love of God in their lives. In discussing infant baptism or dedication services with parents, I find that it is most often the sense of gratitude that comes through as a key reason for wanting a church service, because new parents are so aware that they have received the gift of a child. Our society has gone a long way towards abandoning this concept, perhaps because contraception and abortion both emphasize choice, and therefore control, over the number, timing and health of children in a family. But in reality, conception is still a miraculous process, and the growth of a human being from such 'accidental' beginnings is probably the greatest wonder of the world.

Yet often, we celebrate the gift of new life only in cases where it is seen to be 'against the odds', where our human explanations and rationalizations have run out, and we are forced to look outside ourselves for the source of the miracle. When there have been difficulties along the way, through infertility, miscarriages, or a neonatal death, we rejoice and celebrate when a healthy baby eventually comes along. When the couple are young and healthy, we tend simply to accept a new baby as their automatic right. Because many current medical procedures are costly, we have begun even to accept that people can buy a baby, through IVF, surrogacy or adoption. Thus, as science has offered more and more help to those wanting children, the hidden danger behind the many positive advances is that our concept of a child as a gift has been eroded.

✣

BIBLE FOCUS: FROM ABRAHAM TO ZECHARIAH
PARENTS AGAINST ALL ODDS

Do you know many women who've given birth in their 90s, or many centenarian fathers? Even with the benefit of scientific advances, we have so far only managed to prolong women's fertility into their 60s. The case of a 60-year-old French woman who gave birth to a child fathered by her brother made headlines and raised a host of ethical, moral and health issues. What it did most obviously, however, was to obscure the actual baby in the frenzied fog of international media coverage. Whatever the rights and wrongs of its parenthood, the life of this child was and is a gift, just as were the two sons born to Abraham and Zechariah respectively, in the Old and New Testaments of the Bible.

As a big fan of families, I love the fact that these two unlikely births both herald the dawning of a new age for the people of God. That's how crucial families are to the big picture of God's dealings with humankind. Let's look at Abraham's son first.

A promise kept

God promises Abram (as he was then called) that he will be a father, at the same time as he sends him out from his home country:

The Lord said to Abram: 'Leave your country, your family, and your relatives and go to the land that I will show you. I will bless you and make your descendants into a great nation. You will become famous and be a blessing to others. I will bless anyone who blesses you, but I will put a curse on anyone who puts a curse on you. Everyone on earth will be blessed because of you.'
GENESIS 12:1–3

All this happens when Abram is already 75 years old! The Lord then shows him his future home, in the land of Canaan, and Abram demonstrates his faith in God by building an altar there and then, in the middle of a pagan country. As well as Abram's faith, it is his courage in publicly obeying the Lord that marks him out as the man of God's choice to be the father of his chosen people. Not that he is perfect, however...

Ten years pass, with adventures and deceptions along the way. Abram and Sarai are delivered from their difficulties by the grace of God, and they are, amazingly, brought to live in Canaan, the land God had promised them. Nevertheless, they are beginning to doubt God's promise of children. So, in keeping with contemporary custom, Sarai gives her slave girl to her husband to provide him with an heir. The girl, Hagar, duly becomes pregnant, but falls out with Sarai and is banished from the household. The justice and mercy of God are strikingly seen in the way he meets her on the road, rescues her and promises to provide for her (Genesis 16:7–14).

A further thirteen years pass before God renews his promise to Abram: 'Abram was ninety-nine years old when the Lord appeared to him again and said, 'I am God All-powerful. If you obey me and always do right, I will keep my solemn promise to you and give you more descendants than can be counted' (Genesis 17:1–2).

At the same time, God gives Abram and Sarai their new names—

Abraham and Sarah—and, with their new names, new identities as the father and mother of nations. God also instructs Abraham to circumcise all the men and boys in his family as a sign of their membership of the covenant people of God. Wrestling with the impossibility of Sarah having a child at 90, Abraham bursts out laughing, but tries to hide his doubt by suggesting a feasible alternative—that Ishmael, already thirteen, could inherit God's promise. But God is insistent:

'No! You and Sarah will have a son. His name will be Isaac, and I will make an everlasting promise to him and his descendants... Your son Isaac will be born about this time next year, and the promise I am making to you and your family will be for him and his descendants for ever.
GENESIS 17:19, 21

Sarah, too, laughs, when she meets God in the form of the three visitors who come to their home and repeat God's promise to them. But this story is all about God's love, promise and gift, freely given to Abraham and Sarah, not earned by their faithfulness. So, wonderfully, God does not punish Abraham or Sarah for their lack of faith. Instead, he turns their mocking laughter of disbelief into the laughter of joy at the gift of a son, whose very name means 'laughter'.

His name is John

Many centuries later, Zechariah and Elizabeth are every bit as unlikely to have a baby as their forebears, Abraham and Sarah (Luke 1:5–25). They too are well advanced in years and suffering public shame that God has not blessed them with children. We know little more about them except that they are both from priestly families, and are continuing to obey God's law and worship him.

I've always thought of Zechariah as a rather bumbling and doddery old man, afraid and confused by the sudden appearance of an angel in the temple. I may not be alone in this, but on reflection I do think that Zechariah gets a bad press. I'd certainly be both afraid and confused if I encountered an angel as I walked into church, wouldn't you? And the angel understands exactly how he feels. As usual, whether speaking to Zechariah, Mary, Joseph or the shepherds, Gabriel's first words are, 'Don't be afraid' (Luke 1:13).

He then tells Zechariah that he has been chosen by God to be part of something much bigger than his own family. Yes, his and Elizabeth's prayers will be answered, but there is much more to it than that. This child will be the prophet through whom God announces the long-awaited Messiah. Well, Zechariah knew that this was a special day, because he had been given the rare privilege of being chosen to go into the temple to burn incense, but I doubt he ever dreamt it would be this special. The angel's news is, literally, epoch-making. With hindsight, we can see the full truth of this far more than Zechariah could at the time. Suffice to say, his disbelief is understandable.

Being struck dumb is often thought of as a punishment for the old priest, but in many ways I think it is a blessing. Zechariah is given a space to adjust—to think, pray and fully take on board what he has been told. In our culture, we expect people to react to earth-shattering news very quickly—often, sadly, for the benefit of reporters who want a good soundbite. Adjusting to major changes takes time, however, particularly when people are older. Saul's period of blindness after his conversion was, similarly, a very necessary time of reflection and transition for him.

I expect that Zechariah and Elizabeth lived very privately (and quietly!) for the next nine months, and communicated in many ways other than speech, drawing on the resources of decades of married life together. Mind you, Mary's visit after six months must have come as a welcome end to the imposed silence. More seriously, her visit served to reassure them that God's great plan of salvation was indeed being worked out before their eyes.

John's birth marks the end of the transition for Zechariah and Elizabeth, which is completed at John's naming ceremony, when Zechariah's speech is restored as soon as he writes the crucial words, 'His name is John' (Luke 1:63). They are crucial not only because they seem to unlock Zechariah's tongue, but because they represent

Zechariah's acceptance of God's plan for his family. Just as God has given the child, he has also given the name. So John is a gift from God, a gift which will bring them great joy, but to which they must hold lightly. By stepping outside tradition and family expectations, by *not* naming his son Zechariah, the elderly father is embracing the way of God, as expressed in his wonderful prophecy at the end of Luke chapter 1.

You, my son, will be called a prophet of God in heaven above. You will go ahead of the Lord to get everything ready for him. You will tell his people that they can be saved when their sins are forgiven. God's love and kindness will shine upon us like the sun that rises in the sky. On us who live in the dark shadow of death this light will shine to guide us into a life of peace.
LUKE 1:76–79

❖

IN A NUTSHELL

This chapter has focused on preparing for and adjusting to parenthood. The needs of young families were recognized, and suggestions given as to how family, friends and the local church can best provide support.

As society's view of babies changes, it is important to hold on to the sense of each child as a gift from God, rather than a right or a possession. This was graphically illustrated in the Bible stories of Abraham and Sarah and of Zechariah and Elizabeth, who were 'parents against all odds'.

GROWTH POINTS

- What is your experience of the local church 'being there' (p.35), or not being there, for young families? How could support be improved and strengthened?

- Read again the 'What about Dad?' section on page 37. Do you agree with Sebastian Kraemer's comments? Can the church help fathers today?

- For further Bible study, read Luke 1 all the way through. What insight does it give into God's heart for families? If you are in a group, you could read in parts, with different people taking the roles of Gabriel, Zechariah, Mary and Elizabeth, and two narrators. The narration could be split as follows:
    Narrator 1: vv. 1–4, 26–28a, 29–30a, 34a, 35a, 38a and c, 57–60a, 61–67.
    Narrator 2: vv. 5–13a, 18a, 19a, 21–24, 39–42a, 46a, 56, 80.

CLEARINGS

HAVING OUR TEA

There's something religious in the way we sit
At the tea table, a tidy family of three.
You, my love, slicing the bread and butter, and she,
The red-cheeked tot a smear of blackberry jam, and me.
A new creation is established, a true presence.
And talking to each other, breaking words over food
Is somehow different from customary chatting.[4]

PRAYER

Use the poem above to inspire your prayer. It portrays the delicate balance between the parents' love for each other, their love for their child, and hers for them. Just three people, yet already a complex web of relationships, each strand of which must be strengthened and protected. Give thanks and pray for the web of relationships in a family known to you, remembering especially those strands that are fragile, in need of repair or protection.

NOTES

1. Fergal Keane, *Letter to Daniel*, BBC/Penguin, 1996, pp. 35, 36
2. Sheila Kitzinger, quoted in *The Times*, 10 December 2001
3. Sebastian Kraemer, child and family psychiatrist, Tavistock Clinic, quoted in *The Times*, 7 September 2000
4. Bobi Jones, translated from the Welsh by Joseph Clancey, from *Bobi Jones: Selected Poems*, Dinefwr Press & Publishers

CHAPTER 3

SECOND HELPINGS: THE NEW DYNAMICS OF SIBLING RELATIONSHIPS

'He's better than a best friend: he's my brother!'
CAPTION IN THE FAITH ZONE OF THE MILLENNIUM DOME

BETTER THAN A BEST FRIEND

As we looked up at the life-sized photo on the wall, both the words and the image of two children in a park conveyed a deeply reassuring message. It conveyed the importance of friendship and trust between children, which can first be learned in the family, with their siblings. Children's stories and adult novels frequently focus on the benefits of strong sibling relationships, and the dangers of poor ones, from Jane Austen and George Eliot to Enid Blyton and Arthur Ransome, to many excellent contemporary children's stories by authors such as Jaqueline Wilson. Even in fairy tales, the theme is evident: Hansel and Gretel help and comfort each other, whereas Cinderella's sisters' ugliness is the outward sign of, and maybe even the punishment for, their unkind treatment of her. In fairy tales, after all, the good are invariably beautiful and the bad are ugly.

Double the trouble?

In a family of three, with two parents and one child, there are three relationships between individuals. In a family of four, there are six.

A mathematical friend tells me that the numbers increase in a Fibonacci sequence, so that families of five have 15 one-to-one relationships within them, and families of six have 21. It follows, then, that those living in larger families experience a range of 'group' relationships and learn how to relate to two, three or four siblings, and to people of different ages and genders. We will look later (in Chapter 6) at how this influences the development of each child's identity. For the moment, let us focus on the birth of the second child and its impact on the family unit.

Double the relationships; double the time needed to keep them strong; half the time in which to do it! It is rarely that simple, however. For a start, having a second child is a very different experience from first time around. The second-time parents I talk to at our church's weekly drop-in are all enjoying their second baby more, feeling more relaxed and confident in their role as parents, less likely to compare their child with others of the same age or to worry about their weight, sleep or development. It is clear that many of their previous anxieties and questions have already been answered and they now feel infinitely experienced compared with the time when they were just starting out on parenthood. Parents expect the experiences of birth and babyhood second time around to be broadly similar to the first time, and so face the prospect of a second child with clearer expectations of what the next few months will hold. Of course, illness, disability or other health complications may alter this scenario, and for some parents a second pregnancy and baby may demand great courage as previous difficulties are conquered or new ones encountered.

For mothers who work outside the home, the second baby brings many new challenges, and childcare costs are doubled. As a result, the number of mothers who give up their jobs virtually doubles after the birth of their second child. The financial pressures this places on the family are considerable, as are the stresses of adjustment to full-time motherhood. Some parents decide at this stage to share childcare responsibilities, or to change to the father being home-based, so that the mother can return to her job. Recent research demonstrates that the 'second child syndrome' is a real pressure for parents, but is overlooked by mainstream researchers and policy makers. Sue Clasen, Chair of WATCH (a campaign for greater awareness of children's needs) identifies emotional as well as practical factors:

Many women start to reassess their lives after their second child is born because this is when they begin to recognize their value as mothers. They realize they may have missed out on something very precious first time round. They begin to see that the task of managing two children, a partner and a home can be a satisfying challenge in itself.

Diane Honster, a social psychologist and co-director of the Economic and Social Research Council, explains this trend as being the result of incompatible priorities and inflexible working patterns, rather than women's loss of interest in their careers.[1]

Whatever working arrangements are made, one great advantage now is that parenting manuals can be read with informed interest, rather than being devoured as infallible guides to an unknown planet. It is astounding, however, how little attention is paid to the new dynamic that a second child brings into the family. Where previously there were two types of relationship in place (the partnership between parents and the parent–child relationships), there now exists a third—the relationship between the two children. This is the only bond that does not directly involve an adult and hence, perhaps, the lack of importance given to it in advice for parents. Yet all parents have a dream of their children being best friends for life. An impossible dream, perhaps? I believe it is a dream we must hold on to, because how siblings relate to each other is absolutely crucial for the family as a whole.

In this chapter we will address the impact of parents' and other adults' relationships with siblings. In Chapter 4, we will look more closely at how we can foster the skills and attitudes needed for siblings to relate well to each other. First of all, let's set the scene.

Love–hate

There are two universal assumptions about siblings: they will love each other... and they will hate each other. The paradox is that both are true, for the archetypal love–hate relationship is the one between siblings. This has been well documented by Adele Faber and Elaine Mazlish in their fascinating book, *Siblings without Rivalry*, which makes compulsive reading for parents. They describe two forces at work—one pushing the siblings apart as they use the differences between them to establish themselves as unique individuals, the other drawing them together into their unique bond as siblings.[2] All parents of two or more children watch this paradox being played out every day as siblings fight one minute, hug the next; or disagree violently at lunchtime but laugh together uproariously over supper. Brothers and sisters really bring out the best and the worst in each other: they know 'which buttons to push' to annoy each other, but equally, they can offer each other unconditional sympathy and comfort like no one else can. As one mother of two put it, 'Their fighting is exhausting—but when the chips are down they can be sweet to each other... helpful and supportive.'

Interestingly, in his letter to the Romans, Paul describes not just interpersonal relationships, but the whole human condition, in terms of an inward struggle between the forces of good and evil: 'Even when I want to do right, I cannot. Instead of doing what I know is right, I do wrong' (Romans 7:18–19).

Paul's description takes us to the very heart of sibling relationships, for they are intrinsically linked to the personal, inward battle to conquer our self-centredness and insecurities that faces every human being. Winning the battle is crucial, for the family as a whole, for every individual within it, and for all their future relationships. We need to remember that just as positive family relationships create the environment in which security, love and trust can grow, the very closeness of those same relationships makes them the breeding ground for insecurity, jealousy and hatred.

So let's look now at how the behaviour of adults can strengthen or weaken sibling relationships.

Peas in a pod?

We know that every child is a unique individual, different from any other person in our immediate family, in our wider family—in fact, in the entire world. Yet, as we've seen, parents expect the birth and early months of a second child to be similar to their sibling's, and so there is a tendency to expect the child to behave and react in the same way too. I certainly thought this, and was in for a rude awakening when I realized that our second daughter would not sleep or feed to order, as her sister had done. She not only looked very different but was totally different in personality, and has remained so. Appreciating and celebrating the differences between them has always been immensely challenging and rewarding for us as parents. So, never expect a second child to be like a first; nor, for that matter, subsequent siblings. Thereafter, it's all about encouraging different interests, spotting each child's unique talents and strengths, and allowing them to develop in the way that's right for them.

A while ago, we were delighted to receive a birth announcement card from friends who had just had their second daughter. It boasted a photograph of the sisters together, and included the older child in the wording of the announcement. These wise parents had recognized that the new arrival would impact their first child's life every bit as much as their own, and that it was never too early to start fostering a positive relationship between the siblings.

Gender issues

Most mothers feel pressure to produce children of both genders—small wonder, when the model family of four, with one son and one daughter, is still paraded in many advertisements, TV sitcoms and holiday brochures. By recognizing each child's individuality, it is possible to ease the pressure. Two children of the same sex are likely to be as different in personality as two of the opposite sex, because personality and gender are two very different issues. There are, of course, some issues that confront parents of girls and not of boys, and vice versa, and comparing notes with relatives or friends who share these experiences is very helpful. The most important task for every parent, however, is to get to know each child and nurture, guide and encourage him or her as a unique individual. This responsibility and privilege will be different for each child, whether we have two daughters, three sons or, like bewildered Mr Bennett in *Pride and Prejudice*, five daughters.

When our second daughter was born, alongside our joy at meeting her, there was a sense, in some people's reactions, that I had 'failed' to produce a boy. I was greatly helped by a close friend (and mother of girls) who wrote us a card wishing us as much joy in our girls' bond as sisters as they had known in their family. When we were expecting our third child, the pressure was much less, although several people actually said, 'You must be hoping for a boy this time.' This was simply not the case: we already knew, from having two daughters, that our third child would be unique, regardless of gender.

All this has led me to encourage expectant parents to focus on the positives of same-gender relationships for their children, as well as the positives of having 'the opposite of last time'. It is great for a girl to have a brother, and for a boy to have a sister, but it is also a real bonus for a girl to have a sister or a boy to have a brother. Many adults find these same-sex bonds hugely important: 'We rely on each other for support and to share confidences,' one woman said of her relationship with her younger sister. 'We get on very well—better than ever,' commented a man about his older brother. This is not to say that sister/brother relationships are not equally fulfilling, but there is often more common ground for brothers and sisters to share as they grow up, which makes keeping in touch easier. Certainly, much as our son appreciates having two sisters, he feels the absence of a brother, and he is always keen to spend time with his male cousins of similar ages to compensate for this.

One to one

Each child needs the undivided attention of his or her parents on a regular basis. We will never get to know and understand our children well unless we spend time with them on their own as well as with the rest of the family. In addition, rivalry for parental attention, which often leads to sibling conflict, can be stopped only through giving each child one-to-one time. One father highlighted the need to spend time 'every day with each of them', and later told me how, as a child in a large family, he had only really felt 'equally loved' at bedtime, when his parents said prayers with each child on their own. Another father pointed out the challenge of being there for each child, particularly when, as in his case, the age gaps are quite large: 'You need to work at spending as much time with the youngest as you did with the older ones, which isn't easy as you get older, busier, less interested, etc.'

It's good to bear in mind, however, that we don't need to be doing anything particularly special for our children to benefit. In fact, I heard a preacher once talk about his young children all eagerly volunteering, the minute he said the immortal words, 'Would one of you like to come…?' Long before he'd finished saying where he was going, they sensed the chance of some one-to-one time with him. It may be a walk to nursery, to the postbox, to the shops or park, or reading a story, or doing a jigsaw together—anything, in fact, where the child knows that they have you to themselves, without interruption, for a few minutes. One of my most lasting memories of my father is of an afternoon on holiday when I was six, when I took an endless walk, of maybe half a mile, along the beach with him on my own. Then we stopped at a café where he had a cup of tea and I had a drink of lemonade (in a bottle with a straw—what a treat!) which I made last as long as possible, in order to enjoy his exclusive attention for what felt like hours.

Available—to whom?

These days, constant availability can have its down side for our children. An answerphone is very useful at bedtimes—switching it on tells the child that they are our top priority and everyone else can wait. Conversely, let's be sure that mobile phones do not rob our children of the attention they deserve. Recent newspaper articles have shown the danger to families of workaholic parents who never leave the office behind and even take a mobile and a lap-top on holiday. I fear we are well on the way there: I visited Kew Gardens recently and observed a man speaking on his mobile, his young daughter by his side. He was totally ignoring the world-famous surroundings and also his companion, who can only have felt that the phone call was more important than their time together.

I returned to teaching part-time as our youngest child started school, and I was anxious to collect him at midday whenever possible in the two terms before he went to school full-time. So, four mornings a week, I rushed back from work to the infant school, hoping that the teacher would let them out a few minutes late. Then we'd ride home, with him still just small enough to sit in the child-seat on the back of the bike, and we'd collapse on the sofa together. We always had soup and a sandwich for lunch, because it was quick, filling and easy! I sometimes wondered if it was worth the rush—whether I should have asked someone else to collect him—but I knew the answer. We would never have that time again, and I wanted to make the most of it. My son once said to me, 'Mum, d'you remember when I was in Reception and we used to have soup for lunch, just the two of us...?' Enough said!

Personal space

One expression of each child's individuality is the need for their own space. This becomes more acute as they get older, and is very difficult for many families to provide. When children are under five, sharing a room does not often cause too many problems, although the older one's toys, models and treasured possessions may need to be put out of reach of their little brother or sister. I also think it is important to maintain the status quo and put younger children to bed first, allowing the older ones some privileges, even if this is complicated to achieve. I remember tucking one child up in bed while the next was having a story or watching a video downstairs and the oldest was getting out of the bath; I was fortunate that their father was usually home from work in time to be part of the balancing act. But it is worth it: we can't expect older children to take responsibility later on—for example, with babysitting—if we don't treat them any differently from their younger siblings.

We have juggled every combination of sleeping arrangements, from three children in the same room to each on their own. The children's individual personalities have developed through having a space of their own, and then making the room 'work' for them. Rather like the British TV series *Through the Keyhole*, anyone who knows our children could tell you instantly whose room is whose, the moment they entered it. When separate rooms are totally impossible, it's still worth considering as many creative solutions as possible. One family of three boys did an annual swap-around so that every combination of 'two and one' was experienced, and each boy had a room of his own for one year in three. Interestingly, these brothers have very strong relationships with each other now, in their 20s. Another family built a half-wall to subdivide a large, long bedroom into two separate spaces, which worked well. However small the space, each child needs somewhere to call 'mine'. One of our children's rooms is roughly six feet square, but it's still enough to be 'a room of one's own'.

Sharing bedrooms with siblings is a common memory of many adults, usually reflecting on the problems caused. Often this stemmed from being forced to share with a sibling of the same sex, especially if another sibling of the opposite sex had the luxury of a single room. Also, as children get older, their different personalities often clash over tidiness, colour schemes, music, and anything else you can think of. This mother of four has been acutely aware of her own children's relationships because of her memories of childhood:

We got on pretty well until I had to start sharing a bedroom with my sister! I was ten and she was not quite five. It was tricky through secondary school with homework and different bedtimes. I ended up rushing homework downstairs and reading under the covers for hours. I found my sister very annoying and I resented having to look after her when I felt I should be out with my friends. My brother kept himself very much to himself.

When children are given their own space, and not forced together, they tend to get on much better and choose to spend time together. Our daughters now choose to 'double up' whenever the opportunity arises, and love sharing a tent on holiday. Their brother also sneaks into their rooms (or tent) for a chat, a game of cards, or a midnight feast—to which their parents turn a blind eye, of course. On Christmas morning, they always open their stockings together, on the top bunk in the oldest's bedroom. I suspect they may still be doing this for many years yet, as long as Santa continues to visit.

Never compare...

I am stunned by the number of people I have spoken to who feel that their brothers and sisters were favoured by their parents. Did I just pick all the wayward misfits I know? Or is there a dynamic in parent–child relationships that affects how children view themselves and their siblings? A mother summed up her reflections on sibling relationships with these words: 'I think that if one child thinks they are loved less, this will carry on into adult life and affect the relationship with the one perceived to be more favoured.'

Another parent felt strongly enough about it to quote Shakespeare: 'Comparisons are odious—I feel this is the bottom line!' I remembered this as I listened to a woman who is now a grandmother talking about her late father's inferiority complex, which lasted throughout his life. As the oldest son, he had taken on and run the family business, with great efficiency and success, but he had heard so much about how his younger brother had 'made it' by becoming a bank manager that he felt he could never measure up. In addition, while he'd stayed at home during the war, in a 'reserved' occupation, his brother had won medals and glory, driving tanks. The relationship between the brothers never recovered, and those between their children remain strained to this day.

Then I talked with two sisters who both felt that the other one was favoured. 'Why?' I asked. The answer came back loud and clear from them *both*: 'Because Mum always talks to me about her!' Once these sisters made this discovery, they began to feed back to each other all the positives they heard—all the appreciation, encouragement, pride and empathy that their parent had only ever said to the *other* daughter. The sisters' relationship was transformed as a result, and they resolved to support and encourage each other whenever possible, instead of envying each other's 'favoured' status.

Yet the miscommunication which robbed those sisters of a close relationship for many years could so easily have been avoided. It was not done deliberately, perhaps not even consciously, but as soon as their parent talked to them about another sibling, what they heard was a comparison. Most parents have bitten back the words, 'Your brother/sister would never do/say that', or something similar, but it is more far-reaching than this.

We don't need, as parents, to say 'Your sister is prettier than you'; we only need to say 'Your sister looks lovely' for the other one to feel ugly by comparison. Anything we say to children about their siblings will be felt as a comparison, particularly if we aren't feeding in the positives that each child needs to hear. To summarize, a few tips from a parent of four young adults:

- Making comparisons is tempting but unhelpful.
- Grouching about one to the other is not helpful.
- Affirm each for what they are.
- Be fair.
- Encourage them to listen to each other.

We've considered ways in which parents can celebrate the differences between siblings and nurture them as individuals, but it is also important to help them relate to each other and feel a part of the family unit. In Chapter 5 we will consider aspects of family life that can nurture each individual within it.

Balancing act

The complexity of relationships within a family cannot be overstated. As parents, we need constantly to find the balance between focusing on individuals and on the whole family unit. One parent commented, 'We have always tried to recognize their own strengths and weaknesses, whilst, at the same time, being aware and alert to the needs of others, and to recognize the value of different responses.'

When this tricky balance is achieved, however temporarily, the family will become a dynamic and nurturing community for each of its members. In families where siblings relate well, there is less tension and competition, and the family is more outward-looking, able to include and support others. The fruits of this will be enjoyed for years to come by an ever-increasing family circle. Real life, of course, is rarely that simple, which is why the biblical view of families can offer us much hope when relationships do break down, however seriously. The huge success of the musical *Joseph and his Amazing Technicolour Dreamcoat* has been due not only to its songs but to its very contemporary theme—a family that we would now describe as 'complex' and 'dysfunctional', but through which God chose to rebuild a nation.

✥

BIBLE FOCUS: JOSEPH AND HIS BROTHERS LEARNING TO BE FRIENDS

Daddy's boy

Joseph had one younger brother, Benjamin. Sadly, their mother Rachel died in childbirth, and Jacob, their father, never recovered from his loss. He had fallen in love with her as a young man, but had been tricked by her father into marrying her older sister Leah instead. Leah was the mother of six of Joseph's half-brothers, making them his cousins as well as brothers. Meanwhile, Jacob had also had children by Leah's servant girl Bilhah, and by Rachel's servant girl Zilpah, in accordance with the customs of the time. Thus Joseph had four more half-brothers, and it was these four with whom, as a teenager, he worked in the fields, shepherding. It can't have been a happy family. Jacob's first marriage was forced upon him, his second marred by Rachel's years of childlessness and her jealousy of her 'fruitful' sister Leah. No wonder the half-brothers found it hard to get on together. As we will also see in the next chapter, Jacob's own relationship with his only brother had been characterized by deception from childhood.

The Bible account tells us clearly that Jacob loved Joseph more than any of his sons, and we are given ample reason (but not excuse) for the favouritism. The effects on Joseph were disastrous. The other boys, particularly Zilpah's and Bilhah's sons, hated him and resented their father deeply. They were 'second class' members of the family, whose mothers never enjoyed the status of wives but remained servants, and who had weaker blood ties with the wider family.

Dream on...

Jacob's unfairness had just as negative an impact on Joseph as on his brothers. Jacob's need to be close to Joseph, particularly after Rachel's death, was so strong that the parent–child relationship dominated and damaged the 'horizontal' relationships in his family. Spoiled and indulged, without a mother to share in his parenting, Joseph had no sense of his responsibility towards other family members, no ability to see things from their point of view or to relate to them with respect. He probably felt close only to his elderly father, and perhaps to his much younger brother Benjamin. The result was that 'he was always telling his father all sorts of bad things about his brothers' (Genesis 37:2). The special coat, which makes this story so popular, may or may not have been multicoloured, but it was certainly a vivid and constant reminder of the favouritism that nearly cost Joseph his life. When he started to have extraordinarily vivid dreams, and to share them with his brothers, it was only a matter of time before their jealousy erupted into violence.

Responsible Reuben

Joseph's oldest brother, Reuben, was no paragon, but he had some sense of responsibility as the oldest in the family, and courage too. He also loved his father, but was able to recognize his faults and their effect. He was probably not with the brothers in Dothan when they hatched their plan to kill Joseph and lie to their father, but as soon as he hears about it he voices his opposition. To be outnumbered nine to one cannot have been easy. Reuben manages to persuade them not to kill Joseph, but to put him in a dry well instead, and plans to return later and rescue him. This courageous plan is foiled by Judah, who, seeing a caravan of slave traders in the distance, eyes the chance to make a profit and to ease their consciences. 'What will we gain if we kill our brother and hide his body?' he says. 'Let's sell him to the Ishmaelites and not harm him. After all, he is our brother' (Genesis 37:26–27).

Most of us would not see selling a sibling into slavery as 'not harming' him, nor as a generous option, but in this context it is—until the brothers compound their crime by lying to Jacob about it.

Reuben is not there when Joseph is sold—for the same sum, 'thirty pieces of silver', that Judas received for betraying Jesus. Significantly, when he returns to rescue Joseph and before he knows what has happened, Reuben takes responsibility for his little brother, saying, 'The boy is gone! What am I going to do?' (Genesis 37:30). Only Reuben sees the true horror of what the brothers have done, and the pain it will cause Jacob. The symbol of Joseph's status as favoured son becomes the symbol of his death, as the coat is smeared with goat's blood and taken by the brothers to Jacob. The old man is allowed to believe that his son has been killed by wild animals and is inconsolable. The brothers must have hoped that, once Joseph was out of the way, they would enjoy more of their father's favours, but the reverse is true. His refusal to be comforted by them just underlines the breakdown in relationship with all his other children. 'All Jacob's children came to comfort him, but he refused to be comforted. "No," he said, "I will go to my grave, mourning for my son"' (Genesis 37:35).

Poles apart

Apart from one chapter about the family of Jacob's fourth son, Judah, the Genesis narrative then stays with Joseph for the next twenty years or so of the story, and we don't know what is happening to the old man and his family. Down in Egypt, an astonishing chain of events takes Joseph through the full sequence of Egyptian social status: he is in turn slave, prisoner, overseer, freedman, royal advisor and eventually governor. The most significant changes, however, take place on the inside. First of all, Joseph is forced to cope without his father's pampering, and to look up to and show respect for those over him, rather than always being 'top dog'. He has a crash course in humility, beginning with the stark realization of how much his brothers hate him. Through all this, Joseph learns to trust the God of his father for himself, and to find his security and identity in his own relationship with God. As he faces one personal catastrophe after another, we read, 'the Lord helped him and was good to him' and 'the Lord was with Joseph' (Genesis 39:21, 23). Eventually, Pharaoh himself recognizes the source of Joseph's wisdom and tells his officials to enlist his help in managing the impending famine: 'No one could possibly handle this better than Joseph, since the Spirit of God is with him' (Genesis 41:38).

Put to the test

Thus it is a very different Joseph who meets his brothers when they come to Egypt to buy food. Outwardly, the contrast could not have been greater, from precocious teenage shepherd boy to the most powerful commoner in the most powerful country in their world. No wonder the ten brothers did not recognize him. Inwardly, Joseph is in turmoil, but he decides not to disclose his identity until he has tested his brothers' motives. He accuses them of being spies and puts them in prison for three days. The irony of the brothers' response to his accusations makes the tension in this story almost unbearable: 'We're honest men, and we come from the same family

—we're not spies! Sir, we come from a family of twelve brothers. The youngest is still with our father in Canaan, and one of our brothers is dead' (Genesis 42:11, 13).

Gradually, starting from this evidence of their candour, Joseph becomes convinced that his brothers have changed. He sets them a particular test when he asks them to bring Benjamin to him in Egypt, as proof of their honesty, because this brings back to them forcefully their memories of how they treated Joseph: 'We're being punished because of Joseph. We saw the trouble he was in, but we refused to help him when he begged us. That's why these terrible things are happening' (Genesis 42:21).

While the brothers think that their experiences in Egypt are God's punishment for their past actions, what is actually happening is the outworking of God's rescue plan. Similarly, when Jacob eventually agrees to let Judah take Benjamin back to Egypt with them, he is resigned to losing a son, but entrusts him to God, not knowing that this will be the means by which he regains his lost son (Genesis 43:14).

Family reunion

So Joseph sees Benjamin again, to his great joy. Yet still he sets his brothers one final test. After a feast in his house, they set off for home, only to be pursued and arrested by Joseph's men. A silver cup has been planted secretly in Benjamin's grain sack, and the brothers are distraught. They now feel their responsibility keenly and can imagine their father's pain too. Judah pleads to Joseph for his brother (Genesis 44:18–34), who is so moved by this that he sends his servants out of the room and finally tells his brothers who he is. He also makes it plain that he feels no bitterness or hatred towards them. Rather, he sees God's bigger plan at work, sending him on ahead of them to Egypt to save them from the famine.

The power of forgiveness brings healing and wholeness to the family once more—starting with the crucial 'horizontal' dynamic of the brothers, now allies instead of enemies. The reconciliation of the brothers is followed shortly by Joseph's reunion with his father, Jacob, who is so amazed that he can't believe the news. On his way to Egypt, Jacob encounters God in a dream, for the third time in his life (we will consider the previous two occasions in the next chapter). God restates his promise to Jacob that his descendants will become a nation, and also promises him that Joseph, whom Jacob had sworn to mourn until his death, will be at his side when he dies. Improbably and amazingly, Jacob's family is reunited.

❖

IN A NUTSHELL

Chapter 3 has focused on the changes and challenges for the family with the birth of a second child. We looked briefly at the 'love–hate' sibling dynamic, then considered how parents and others can promote good relationships between siblings.

Suggestions for this were celebrating difference, providing one-to-one time for each child, being available, giving individual space, and not comparing siblings with each other.

The story of Joseph and his brothers highlights the need for honest and responsible relationships between siblings, and the possibility of healing and forgiveness by God's grace.

GROWTH POINTS

- What was your experience as a child of how adults helped or hindered your relationship with siblings? Do any of the suggestions in this chapter throw light on these experiences?

- Look again at the section 'Available—to whom?' (p. 52). Use it as a stimulus to consider your own availability to the children in your care.

- Think of one sibling relationship between children which you know well. Use it in your private thinking, or share it with the group, as a case study for the principles of 'celebrating difference' and valuing each individual.

- For further Bible study, read Genesis 45, in which Joseph finally discloses his true identity to his brothers. Imagine you are one of the brothers and describe your feelings. What does this passage show us about the value of healthy sibling relationships?

CLEARINGS

Some day when my children are old enough to understand, I will tell them:

I loved you enough to ask where you were going, with whom and what time you would get home.

I loved you enough to make you return a Mars bar—with a bite out of it—and to confess, 'I stole this.'

I loved you enough to let you see hurt, disappointment, disgust and tears in my eyes.

I loved you enough to admit when I was wrong and ask your forgiveness.

I loved you enough to let you stumble, fall, hurt.

I loved you enough to give you increasing responsibility for household jobs and to train you to do them well.

But most of all, I loved you enough to say NO when you hated me for it—that was hard for me.[3]

PRAYER

Father, give us your love for our children.
Love which is strong but kind,
Tough but compassionate,
All-embracing but personal.
Thank you for loving us in this way.

NOTES

1 Sue Clasen quoted and Diane Honster referred to by Rebecca Andrews, 'Double the Struggle', from *Three Shoes, One Sock and No Hairbrush*, Cassell, 2001 (excerpt published in *The Times*, 21 October 2001)
2 See A. Faber and E. Mazlish, *Siblings without Rivalry*, Piccadilly Press, 1998, p. 13
3 Anonymous, quoted in *The Fives to Fifteens Basic Parenting Programme: Leader's Guide*, Family Caring Trust, 1996

CHAPTER 4

WHEN THE BOUGH BREAKS: SIBLING RIVALRY, FAIRNESS AND FORGIVENESS

Where does it say family life is supposed to be easy? ... It is unrealistic to think happy, cohesive families just happen... The family is the most powerful environmental factor in shaping the personality of the child. If we are going to raise healthy children we need healthy families in which to do it.[1]

WHOSE FAULT?

Older child gets it wrong; younger child gets it right—a familiar tale? Older brother forgets to clear away toys as asked; meanwhile, little sister not only puts hers away, but makes sure that her parent knows she has done so—and that he hasn't. Likely outcome? Older brother gets into trouble and blames little sister, who isn't responsible for his failure to put away his toys, but is definitely the closest person to hit, shout at or put down. The downward spiral begins, and a layer is added to the heap of sibling resentment when the initial problem could have been resolved. 'You've still got time to tidy up and have a bedtime story if you're quick. Would you rather I helped you or timed you? How fast d'you think we could get this done?' Note that there is no mention of little sister in this: the parent deals directly with the older brother.

The phrase 'taking the bait' is used in parenting courses to describe how easily parents can be sidetracked from the central issue, often in order for children to deflect blame or punishment away from themselves on to somone else, typically a sibling. This happens because when children feel bad about themselves, they are unable to think clearly and they try to get attention, to control what's happening, in the hope that this will make them feel good again. 'But try not to take that bait! It won't make them happy; you may only reward the misbehaviour and reinforce it! Try doing the opposite instead, the opposite to what you normally do.'[2]

Adults need great wisdom to avoid being drawn into the blaming process, and to stick to the basic issue on each occasion. It is vital to teach children, by example and encouragement, to take responsibility for their own actions and mistakes rather than looking for someone else to blame. In our society, this is a very unpopular thing to teach, because we live in a 'blame culture'. This culture is now threatening to stop school trips taking place, as teachers are being blamed and sued for tragic accidents, facing trial by media. I read an article written shortly after a railway disaster, which pointed out how, when anything major goes wrong, the search is immediately on for someone to blame. Many people are frightened to admit fault—to tell the truth, in fact—in case they are sued as a result. 'I find that a very worrying situation to be in,' the piece concluded, 'where people are encouraged to invent any excuse rather than say "Sorry, I/we got it wrong."'[3]

Always apologize?

So how do we foster in our children the ability to say 'sorry'? From playgroup to nursery to primary school and beyond, parents and carers feel embarrassed by their children's behaviour. I well remember how I felt when the playgroup leader took me aside to tell me about that morning's 'incident'. It can be quite a shock when we realize that our child is not the 'little angel' her T-shirt proclaims her to be, not the innocent party in every dispute, but quite capable of hitting, biting, pushing, not sharing or throwing a huge tantrum.

The temptation will always be to settle for superficial repentance and apologies. It's easier, but I believe it is dangerous to do so, because in the end it undermines our children's integrity. Making the child 'say sorry' satisfies the adult social code, but has no effect on the child's behaviour. In fact, it actually gives the message that, as long as you say what is expected, it doesn't matter what you think and feel. Do we want to establish this as a pattern of behaviour in the young? Jesus castigated the religious leaders of his day for exactly this: 'Outside you look good, but inside you are evil and only pretend to be good' (Matthew 23:28).

Let us not pretend, either, that children themselves are taken in by forced or throwaway apologies. One of our children had had a tussle in the playground, during which another child had hit him. It could just as easily have happened the other way round, I knew. The culprit was told to apologize, and the matter was settled, as far as their teacher was concerned. But as we walked home that day, I heard how meaningless my son had felt the apology to be. 'I'd rather he didn't say sorry at all than do it because he was told to, because then all that happens is that he blames me for getting him into trouble... I didn't tell on him, but anyone could see the mark where he hit me and I wasn't going to lie about what happened.' The forced apology had only added to the complications in the relationship between the two children.

Bridge building

It is not easy, but it is extremely valuable, for children, especially siblings, to work through their differences and learn to respect and accept each other. Sadly, however, parents can get in the way by not allowing this to happen. There is a strong sense for parents that our children should relate well, and also that how they get on reflects positively or negatively on the parents themselves. Perhaps this is why we put pressure on children to 'be nice—(s)he's your brother/sister'. It is painful to hear or see children arguing, but they need this experience to equip them for life. As Faber and Mazlish put it, siblings learn about friendship through their differences: 'Even if their personalities were such that they never could be friends, at least they would have the power to make a friend and be a friend.'[4]

Accepting the differences between children can be very painful for a parent, but it is an investment for the future, as this parent of teenage sons reflects:

I know that the differences in interests and temperament that kept them from being close in childhood are still there. But I also know that over the years I had helped them build the bridges to span the separate islands of their identities. If they ever need to reach each other they have many ways of getting there.[5]

Forgiveness and the family

Sometimes, more often than we adults choose to admit, interference can make matters more complicated. To ask a child to apologize to their sibling for the sake of short-term harmony may actually do more harm than good. We want our children to be honest about their feelings: if we demand an instant, superficial apology when they are still feeling angry and frustrated, this honesty is completely undermined. It is better by far to give the child time to cool off, reflect on their actions and offer an apology as and when they feel ready to do so. Once they stop feeling pressured, children are well able to respond appropriately, as long as there is a climate in the family of genuinely 'saying sorry and making up' or, in spiritual terms, repentance and forgiveness.

Children can sense and see the effect of this climate on all our family relationships. They can then learn that it takes time, effort, give-and-take, apologies and forgiveness to resolve arguments. An apology is not a magic spell to be applied in the hope that it will make everything better. It's part of a two-way process and has to be accepted, and forgiveness granted, in order to put the relationship right. The most effective way of children learning this is from their parents' and other adults' example. If parents apologize to each other, and to their children, when they make mistakes, children will learn to do so too. If parents' first reaction to an apology is to appreciate the courage and honesty of the child in giving it, then that child will continue to apologize. If, on the other hand, an apology is brushed off with a quick 'That's OK, or 'It doesn't matter', the child learns that apologizing is not worth the effort.

Tough love

It is more important to be responsible parents than popular ones. The strategy often known as 'tough love' means allowing children to take responsibility for their own lives, and to make mistakes along the way. This will be painful at times, for them and their parents, but is vital to children's development. What matters is that children learn and grow, not that we score points over them. But how often do parents, teachers and other adults today still give children the message that they 'always know best'? Or, as I once saw on a poster of a giraffe looking down on a rather feeble rabbit, 'There are two sides to every argument: my side and the wrong one.'

Alternatively, as we have seen, it is all too easy for parents to give in to their children's every whim, to keep them happy, and to protect them from problems rather than allowing them to learn through them. If we can navigate a course between these two extremes, our children will grow in maturity as their self-confidence and sense of responsibility develop.

Native Americans would allow their children to touch a fire, knowing that one painful experience would teach them for ever to be careful, far more effectively than verbal warnings or nagging. Once the lesson was learnt, they could offer comfort and sympathy, and I'm sure they didn't turn round and blame their children or call them stupid for making a mistake. We all know that experience is a great teacher, but our children are unlikely to take our word for things as they grow older: they will have to find out for themselves. Mark Twain famously commented that when he was fourteen, his father knew nothing, but at 21, he found it astonishing how much the old man had learned in seven years!

Not worth the risk

There may be some cases, however, where the danger involved is too great to expose children to this risk. We have some friends who live very near to an electrical substation. Their son, like ours, spent his primary schooldays playing football at every opportunity. It was very likely that one day, their ball would land on the wrong side of the fence, next to the generator. As I walked past with my son one day, I was thinking about this, and about the tragic death of a local child who fell on the live rail of a railway line. Divine inspiration led me to 'do a deal' with my son. 'If your ball ever lands in there,' I told him, 'come and tell me straight away. I promise not to be cross with you for losing your ball, and I promise I will buy you a new one there and then.' This unusually generous offer of a new football made a great impression on him, and over the years, the local river and one or two other dangerous landing places have been added to the list and the offer repeated. I hope our son is learning that there are some risks that are never worth taking, and that we will make it as easy as we can for him to step back from them.

When I was in my early 20s, I borrowed my mother's car to drive some distance to meet a friend one evening. Weather conditions were not good and on the way home I had a collision in the fog. I was driving too fast, with the over-confidence of young people behind the wheel. No one was hurt, but I arrived home badly shaken, in a car that needed several hundred pounds' worth of repairs to the bodywork. Of course, I was somewhat nervous of telling my mother, but I knew from experience that she would probably be fair and supportive. Her first response was concern for me, a big hug, a drink and a listening ear as I poured out to her what had happened.

Once I was calmer, we talked practicalities. We agreed, as my father would have said, that 'worse things happen at sea', but that I was responsible for the damage to the car and the expense and inconvenience caused. She didn't want to claim on insurance and lose her no-claims discount but, as a student, I had no income. (Thankfully, in those days, I didn't have a loan to repay either.) So we agreed that my mother would pay the bills now and I would repay her monthly from my first year's salary, which I began to earn later that year. It was a fair arrangement: it taught me to drive more cautiously and to live with the consequences of my mistakes. The accident was never referred to between us again, my mother never blamed me or used it as a lever to control me, nor did she ever refuse to lend me her car. I have often had cause to be grateful for her responsible parenting and all it taught me.

It's not fair!

Children's sense of what is fair seems inbuilt, particularly when it comes to parental attention. It is amazing how young this starts, and it is simply impossible to be fair in terms of treating children in precisely the same way. Fairness is less to do with accuracy than with perception. If a child feels that something is unfair, no amount of factual proof to the contrary will change their mind. Rather, if the 'unfairness' is recognized and explained, the child will often cope with it with astonishing maturity. One father put it like this: 'Fairness always needs explanation!' The older sibling of a disabled brother commented, 'My parents... would take great care to explain and re-explain why he needed "special" treatment, and generally talked with me honestly and as an adult to make sure I understood why life was often unfair.'

Talking, explaining, discussing and compromising are the tools that work best in helping children to feel that parents are fair, or at least that they're trying to be so. But if one or both parents adopt a 'do as you're told, I'm not going to discuss it!' approach, then the sense of unfairness may persist into adulthood and mar both sibling and parent–child relationships. Many people remember resentment of a sibling, which was frequently triggered by a parent insisting that a younger one was allowed to join in an activity with an older sibling. Similarly, older siblings voiced resentment when they perceived parents to be unfair, usually through more lenient treatment of younger siblings. One family who responded to my enquiries discovered that their son resented his younger sister, but that just discussing issues with him improved all their relationships straight away.

When children are younger, awareness of the potential problem is key, and distraction works wonders. Inviting friends to play with both or all children on the same day may prevent one from feeling left out. When our children were little, I'd try to take the opportunity of some individual time with one of them—for example, playing a game together or making a cake—while the others were playing with friends. Even half an hour of such an activity would transform their outlook, as they saw the hidden benefit to them, and that they'd done something their siblings hadn't. On many occasions I didn't manage this, of course, and there were tears and tantrums. But eventually we reached an agreement that siblings were not allowed to join in when friends came round, unless they were invited to do so. As long as we enforced this consistently, and made sure that the frequency of friends' visits was roughly fair to each of them, it worked. I still remember the jealousy I felt as a child when my older brother played with a friend in preference to me, but also the joy of being included with the older ones on the occasions when they did invite me to join in their games.

Camel or ostrich?

It is certain that, despite our best efforts to encourage positive sibling relationships, anger and resentment will surface. When they do, there are two immediate options for parents. Number one is the camel approach—plenty of noise, blustering and complaining, but no serious action (ask anyone who has tried to ride a camel to verify this!). We assert our authority to forbid the conflict in extreme terms —'Don't ever let me hear you/see you saying/doing that again!'— and then return to what we were doing. This has no effect whatever in the long term. If we're lucky, it might make a difference at the time, but even this is unlikely. In addition, the camel approach sets up a confrontation between the parent and the children, and the parent will be far more stressed and exhausted than anyone else by it: children's ability to let nagging roll off them, like water off a duck's back, is legendary.

Option number two is the ostrich approach, in which the adult chooses to ignore sibling arguments by turning up the volume on the television or radio and concentrating on the newspaper or a good book till the racket dies down. The ostrich approach also entails not hearing (or pretending not to hear) unkind comments or sarcastic side-swipes between siblings. Pleas from one to reprimand the other fall on deaf ears, and only drastic outcomes such as the crash of breaking glass or the sight of blood will elicit any response. This second approach is as ineffectual as the first, with the added danger that the children will simply conclude that their parent doesn't understand or, worse, doesn't care.

The possible consequences of taking the camel or ostrich approaches are these: either the anger will be buried, only to fester and resurface, possibly even years later, or eventually there will be real injury, emotional or physical, to one or both of the siblings. The relationship between them may be damaged for many years. A significant proportion of the people I questioned can remember their parents having siblings with whom they 'didn't get on' and from whom they were thus estranged as adults, often because of a long-forgotten disagreement in childhood.

Honesty is the best policy

Clearly, sibling rivalry is part of the human condition, instinctive and very hard to counter. So what *can* parents and other adults do? Certainly not pretend that everything is fine and tensions do not exist. If we continually paper over the cracks or brush issues under the carpet, we will end up with a home which is a major health and safety risk to all who live there. We have seen that it is much easier constantly to intervene, direct and discipline children than it is to practise 'tough love' and teach responsibility and independence. Similarly, it is easier to ignore sibling rivalry (and hope, unrealistically, that children will grow out of it at some unspecified stage in the future), than it is to acknowledge the tensions and work through them. But working through the difficulties will take time and energy, not knee-jerk reactions to sibling fights or desperate pleas above the noise of sibling arguments.

In *Siblings without Rivalry*, some fascinating conclusions are drawn from the parents' groups discussing the conflict between siblings. Essentially, it emerged that insisting upon good feelings between children (for example, through forced apologies) led to bad feelings, but allowing for bad feelings between children led to good feelings. Simply acknowledging children's feelings, through listening to and affirming them, was found to be very helpful. At times, children would also need to have their hurtful actions stopped, or to be shown how to express their angry feelings acceptably.[6]

Clear communication

All this is dependent on positive communication within the family. We need to keep the communication channels open with our children, by listening, empathizing and interpreting, so that when problems arise it is possible to talk them out within an existing framework of good communication. Family rituals are really important here, be they mealtimes, bathtimes, bedtimes, or walks with the dog. It is vital to have times and places where two or more family members habitually discuss what is going on for them at the moment. Talking with a father of young adults the other day, he expressed his fondness for driving through Richmond Park. He remembered many times listening to his son when he was a teenager, and the 'scenic route' which had provided the opportunity to catch up with what was really concerning him.

These 'parallel' situations, where we can listen and talk without having to make eye contact, are especially helpful with teenage children. Talking through problems one to one is possibly the most exhausting aspect of parenting. If we neglect it, however, we miss the opportunities to teach our children key skills for life—listening, understanding and co-operation. These skills, if acquired, will be an invaluable resource for all their relationships for the rest of their lives. Parenting like this is hard work, but it is work which is very close to the heart of God—part of his kingdom plan for humanity. As one parenting course puts it:

Just as shouting, interrupting, hitting, cursing, and criticizing teaches children to shout, interrupt, hit, curse and criticize, in the same way your gentleness, firmness, honesty, listening, asking forgiveness and encouraging teaches them to be gentle, to be firm, to be honest, to listen, to ask forgiveness and to encourage in turn.[7]

If siblings were programmed to like, consider and share with each other automatically, family life would be a lot less stressful, but our children would be far less prepared for adult life or to relate to those outside the immediate family. One woman reflected on how difficult she found it to live under the same roof as her sister as a child, because 'we had not developed the maturity to accept each other's differences'. As adults, she continued, 'we celebrate our differences and our characters complement each other so we value each other's counsel'.

In a similar vein, an oldest sibling in a large family described the healthy conflict which was part of her childhood: 'We laughed and played well. We also argued and fought. I think that to be healthy, as we are all individuals and need to work out what is the right path to follow. We learned to trust each other, even if we disagreed with each other's decisions.'

⁘

BIBLE FOCUS: FROM CAIN TO JACOB
RIVALRY AND RECONCILIATION

In the beginning...

Sibling rivalry is no modern phenomenon. It has been around almost as long as marital strife. We read of Adam and Eve's first argument in the Bible in Genesis 3, and in the very next chapter comes the account of how Cain kills his younger brother Abel. The world's first family is ripped apart by fratricide. Cain is banished from the presence of the Lord and the protection of his parents, and sent east of Eden, leaving Adam and Eve to bury his brother and mourn their double loss.

We don't know much about Adam and Eve's family, except that they were living outside of Eden and working hard rather than enjoying the extravagant delights of the Garden. We can assume that there were more than a few backward glances towards Eden, causing regrets, accusations and resentments to build up, so that Cain and Abel grew up in the shadow of their parents' fall from grace, taking on the sense of guilt, fear and failure that accompanied it. There may well have been tensions between the brothers, not least because Cain had to labour on the land while Abel had the less arduous task of tending the flocks.

Be this as it may, the Bible account (Genesis 4:1–16) implies that Cain kills Abel, not in retaliation for anything Abel has done to him but because of his own mistakes. Cain fails to give God the first fruits of the fields, God challenges him about it and, instead of admitting his fault and correcting it, Cain lashes out at the nearest target, his younger brother. Abel, meanwhile, has found favour with God because he has given him the firstborn of his flock, and this compounds Cain's sense of his own guilt. Cain vents his anger on his brother, losing the inward battle to which God has already alerted him:

What's wrong with you? Why do you have such an angry look on your face? If you had done the right thing, you would be smiling. But you did the wrong thing, and now sin is waiting to attack you like a lion. Sin wants to destroy you, but don't let it!'

GENESIS 4:6–7

Looking after Number One

As he walks back from the field in which he has murdered his brother, Cain is confronted by God again, who simply asks him where Abel is. Cain's guilty over-reaction is legendary: 'Am I my brother's keeper?' or, in modern parlance, 'How should I know? Am I supposed to look after my brother?' (Genesis 4:9). This response identifies the crux of the story for us. Cain *is* supposed to look after his brother, to be loyal to him, trust and support him, because of the family ties between them. Yet somehow, responsibility has been replaced by rivalry, and empathy by anger. The self-centred, insecure and guilty part of Cain has won through, at the expense of any consideration for his brother or parents. Cain's entire life is blighted from here on, and no redemption is possible for him, only a half-life wandering away from his home and family.

Even in such desperate circumstances as these, however, there is a foretaste of God's mercy and redemption. Some years later, Adam and Eve have a third son, Seth, 'in place of Abel', who in turn has a son. So Adam's line, seemingly devastated, is reinstated. 'About this time,' we read, 'people started worshipping the Lord' (Genesis 4:25–26). Not only the first nuclear family, but the family of God, is restored. And this is a crucial part of the dynamics of families in God's eyes: the restoration of the family goes hand in hand with the spiritual health of the whole people. Several chapters further on in the book of Genesis, we read about another family with problems, whom God rescues.

History repeats... but God rescues

You may know the story of how Jacob, the younger twin, bought his older brother's birthright for a bowl of stew (as I now understand it—I was puzzled for years as a child as to why a 'mess of pottage' should be so attractive). Esau is not forced into this sale; he simply agrees to it because he is hungry. We are also told that he despised his birthright (Genesis 25:19–34). Clearly, both sons are at fault here, but so too must be their parents, who have failed to teach them to value their family traditions and inheritance. Rebekah and Isaac's favouritism, his of Esau and hers of Jacob, has set the boys against each other, fuelling the natural competitiveness between them.

This unhappy rivalry reaches its nadir when Jacob, helped by his mother, tricks his father into giving him the blessing reserved for the firstborn (Genesis 27:1–45). Isaac is growing old, his sight is failing and the light of his life growing dim. There is a feeling of utter despair when he realizes the deception and speaks to Esau:

'Isaac started trembling and said, "Then who brought me some wild meat just before you came in? I ate it and gave him a blessing that cannot be taken back"'(Genesis 27:33).

Now Isaac is unable to bless Esau, and he feels that he has lost both sons as well as his faith in his wife, and he is simply waiting to die. Rebekah has lost the trust of her husband and is terrified that Esau will kill Jacob. Jacob flees for his life to Uncle Laban, who turns out to be as scheming as Rebekah. And Esau? Well, we probably understand the depths of his resentment as we read, 'Esau hated his brother Jacob because he had stolen the blessing that was supposed to be his. So he said to himself, "Just as soon as my father dies, I'll kill Jacob"' (Genesis 27:41).

All four family members are in desperate straits and the family unit is shattered. There is only one chink of light to be seen in this situation: Esau cares enough for his father to decide not to kill Jacob until after Isaac has died. God only needs a chink to allow grace to come into our lives. So, amazingly, Isaac's life is spared for a further twenty years, and Esau's anger is acknowledged and dealt with.

During these years, we see the remarkable working of God's

mercy and forgiveness in mending the broken family. By the time Jacob returns to his homeland and his family, he has had many years of working for Laban in which to reflect on his previous actions, and to learn to trust and obey God rather than reacting in anger each time Laban cheats him. He acknowledges that all he now has—wives, children and livestock—has been given to him by God and is not the result of his own skill or cunning.

Jacob is also realistic enough to see that, after what he did to Esau, Esau might not be very pleased to see him. So he sends a messenger on ahead, and divides his household in the hope that one half might be able to escape if things turn nasty. Then word arrives that Esau is coming out to meet him, with four hundred men. 'An army,' thinks Jacob, as all his worst fears surface. He is fully expecting his brother to attack him and exact revenge. At this point, he could flee in panic, but instead he remembers God's promise to him and prays instead for God to protect and rescue him:

You, Lord, are the God who was worshipped by my grandfather Abraham and by my father Isaac. You told me to return home to my family, and you promised to be with me and make me successful. I don't deserve all the good things you have done for me, your servant. When I first crossed the Jordan, I had only my walking stick, but now I have two large groups of people and animals. Please rescue me from my brother. I am afraid he will come and attack not only me, but my wives and children as well. But you have promised that I would be a success and that some day it will be as hard to count my descendants as it is to count the stars in the sky.
GENESIS 32:9–12

Jacob sends Esau a large gift of choice livestock to demonstrate his wholehearted desire to make amends. The size of the gift shows Jacob's recognition of how much pain and suffering his actions have caused; it also shows how far God has changed him from being grasping and tight-fisted to being generous and open-handed. That night, as Jacob lies down to sleep, head and heart full of his impending reunion with Esau, he meets God face to face and wrestles with him. This is Jacob's second significant encounter with God at night, and again takes place at a time of great tension in his relationship with his brother. Let us backtrack a little to consider the first.

That first night, Jacob had just deceived Esau and broken the relationship between them, so he was running away from home. At that lowest of low points in his life, God stopped him and showed him what seemed then to be an impossible vision of the future, not just for his family but for all humankind:

I am the Lord God who was worshipped by Abraham and Isaac. I will give to you and your family the land on which you are now sleeping. Your descendants will spread over the earth in all directions... Your family will be a blessing to all people. Wherever you go, I will watch over you, then later I will bring you back to this land. I won't leave you—I will do all I have promised.
GENESIS 28:13–15

God's amazing promise remained with Jacob throughout his time away from his homeland, as his prayer in chapter 32 shows.

Now, on this crucial reunion eve, a second encounter serves to confirm God's plans for Jacob. He is given a new name, Israel (which means 'he struggles with God') because 'You have wrestled with God and with men, and you have won' (Genesis 32:28). The new name encapsulates the change that God has brought about in Jacob's life. The man who was born grasping his older brother's heel (the name Jacob means 'grasping' and 'deceiver') has been reborn as he is grasped by God and empowered by him. All the difficulties of his family relationships are an integral part of who Jacob—now Israel—is. Indeed, he has matured through them into the man through whom God will establish the twelve tribes of the nation of Israel. Significantly, the reunion of the brothers is the central event in the healing of the family unit and of all the individuals in it.

Jacob leaves Peniel ('face of God') at sunrise to rejoin his household. He looks up and immediately sees Esau coming towards him. In human terms, Jacob is unprepared for the meeting as he hurriedly organizes his family. In God's sight, however, he is totally prepared, by his experience of the previous night and of the previous twenty years. Like the prodigal son, Jacob bows down to ask forgiveness, but Esau runs out to meet him, embraces him and welcomes him home. What a reconciliation! There is much more to come, because once Jacob and Esau are reconciled, all the other family relationships can be restored as well. Most significantly, Jacob goes to see his father, who is now 180 years old. When Isaac finally dies, reunited with both his sons, they bury him together (Genesis 35:27–29).

In the account of Jacob and Esau's reconciliation, we witness how the hatred, separation and despair of all the intervening years are replaced by love, trust and hope. Where there was darkness in the family, there is light. For those who face desperate family situations, the story shows us that the humanly impossible can happen. God can break in to mend broken hearts, lives and families and to restore his whole people.

❖

IN A NUTSHELL

In Chapter 4 we looked in more detail at sibling rivalry and its causes. We noted how blame and forced apologies can damage sibling relationships, whereas 'tough love' and fairness can make a constructive difference. Adults' response to sibling arguments is crucial: the 'camel' and 'ostrich' approaches were outlined. Honesty and good communication in the family are vital, as the story of Jacob and Esau demonstrates.

GROWTH POINTS

- Do you recognize the scenario described as 'taking the bait' (p. 65)? Think of a specific occasion when you took the bait and replay the situation without taking the bait. In a group, pairs could role-play each other's situation. (It is often helpful for a parent to take their child's part.)

- Think of examples of 'tough love', or the lack of it, that you have experienced. What can you learn from them?

- 'Life's not fair, but it's good!' Do you agree with this maxim? How does your answer affect your dealings with children?

- For further Bible study, read the story of Jacob and Esau in Genesis 27, 32 and 33. What clues do you find that God's mercy and grace are at work in the brothers' relationship?

CLEARINGS

BIROS EVERYWHERE

In the pity of serendipity
I recall my kid brother finding
a biro in the street when no one else
at school had one yet.

Then he was accused of stealing it when
I knew he hadn't but when I was
asked I said he had because of envy
and he got into trouble.

It was like a gift he had of finding
things that I didn't but I do now
looking back and biros everywhere
pointing at me to say sorry.[8]

PRAYER

God of the past, the present and the future,
Forgive us our mistakes
And free us from the power they hold over us.
May we go forward in hope.
Amen

NOTES

1 Tom and Adrienne Frydenger, *Stepfamily Problems*, Spire, 1997, pp. 107, 122
2 Michael and Terri Quinn, *What Can a Parent Do?* Family Caring Trust, 1997, p. 15
3 Revd Neil Evans, in the parish magazine of All Hallows Church, Twickenham, March 2001
4 Adele Faber and Elaine Mazlish, *Siblings without Rivalry*, Piccadilly Press, 1999, p. 12
5 Faber and Mazlish, p. 13
6 Faber and Mazlish, p. 30
7 Michael and Terri Quinn, p. 50
8 Barrie Armstrong, unpublished; used by kind permission of the author

CHAPTER 5

ROOTS AND SHOOTS: THE FAMILY AS A NURTURING COMMUNITY

Lord, what can you make of me?
I am only a twig. Make me a log.
I am only a piglet. Make me a hog.
I am only a letter. Make me a word.
I am only an egg. Make me a bird.
I am only a leaf. Make me a tree.
I am only a drop. Make me a sea.[1]

BACK TO SCHOOL

Remember those first science experiments at school? If you're as old as me, your primary school didn't do 'Science'—it was probably called 'Nature Study'. This is the present-day equivalent:

- Take two plastic cups and fill them with soil.
- Make a hole with your finger in the soil and put a bean in it, then cover the bean over with soil.
- Put one cup on the window sill and the other in a dark place, such as the back of a cupboard. What happens?

Similar experiments compare what happens to the beans in soil that is dry, moist, or soaking wet. We might also try putting one bean in the fridge, another in the school boiler room and another in the classroom. The children will observe and draw what happens and there will be a range of results—from strong, healthy bean plants to leggy, yellowing specimens, to completely lifeless cups of soil.

What do children learn from this scientific exploration? The answer is that all plants need light, moisture and warmth to grow. Too little, or too much, of any of these requirements will inhibit the plant's growth, or stop it all together. The experiments assume, of course, that we provide a cup of soil in which the bean is planted—the right 'medium' for growth. With cress seeds, cotton wool does the job just as well, but no seed will grow in mid-air!

The medium in which our children grow from infancy, and in which they discover their identity, is the family. The conditions children need—the light, moisture and warmth—are time, encouragement and unconditional love. We will consider these in order, and in the next chapter we will look at how the child's position in the family in relation to their siblings can also influence their development, self-esteem and ability to relate to others.

First of all, some thoughts on time—the 'light' of the family growing medium.

SLOW: CHILDREN

The huge white letters across the road outside the school have a message not only for drivers, but for all who live and work with children. In the rat-race of modern life, children are very vulnerable. They get caught up in adults' over-busy, over-stressed lifestyle. Not that this is a new phenomenon: spending time with children has not been a high priority for parents down the centuries. In the 17th century, Izaac Walton wrote of a day spent fishing with his son as 'a day wasted'. Yet there are no short cuts in parenting, and we need to slow down enough to move at our children's pace, not to make them fit into our agendas or timescales. If we don't slow down, it will simply be too late: our children will have grown up and gone.

One of the hardest but most important things to teach our children is how to wait. Over the years, there are many things we can do with them to encourage this ability. If we say prayers with them, perhaps at bedtime or as a grace before meals, we can also help them see the answers, over the next few days, weeks, months or even years. Anything creative that takes time to plan or prepare helps to build the sense that good things are worth waiting for and often take time to develop. Making presents for Christmas or birthdays gives tremendous enjoyment, the time taken being as much a part of the present as the finished article. Gardening is also wonderful for this, whether it's cress that sprouts on the kitchen windowsill next day or a bowl of bulbs planted in autumn to flower in spring. Gradually, our children develop a longer-term perspective and can see beyond the present moment; this affects their behaviour and, later, their decision-making.

It is also important for parents to take time to make decisions, and not to be rushed into them by our children. It can be useful to explain this:

- 'I can't concentrate on this now while I'm cooking, but could we talk about it at bedtime?'
- 'I need to think more about this. I'll let you know as soon as I can.'
- 'I'd like to discuss this with your mother, so we'll get back to you in good time for you to make your arrangements.'

In Chapter 7, we will look more closely at decision-making with children as they get older. There needs to be a shift in adult thinking so that parents can accept that teenagers' time is their own, not their parents'. Habits of respect and understanding need to be developed, in order to affirm teenagers and the uniqueness of their individual experiences. But it starts further back in time.

Golden days

Think of your own childhood and your happiest memories of it. I suspect that, like me, you might remember days on holiday, special places or occasions, or simple times of feeling close to other family members or friends, when time seemed to stand still and the sun was always shining. Was it really like that, I wonder? Maybe not exactly, but the sense of having time is the golden thread that weaves happy memories together for me.

There was the day my brother and I went sea-fishing with our father off the west coast of Ireland, leaving in the morning and returning after dark. We spent the last hour of the voyage home huddled next to Dad in the tiny cabin, me wrapped in his jacket to keep warm, eating squares of rich dark chocolate (which I can still taste as I write this, over thirty years later). Even on a rough sea, when others on board were fishing for sharks, I felt safe because my father and older brother were there. Most of all, in my ten-year-old thoughts, that exciting, daring, extraordinary day seemed to go on for ever. We want to be those who help create these golden memories for the children in our care. But there are no short cuts: it takes time.

You're only young once

Another crucial aspect of the need for time in our families is the sense of allowing our children to be children and not rushing them through their childhood. Much recent research shows that children's educational progress is better when they start their formal schooling later, as in Scandinavia, and it is important for parents and those working with young children to take note and stand against the trend to push children at a very young age. A child of five has just passed a GCSE in Maths: I am delighted for him and his proud parents, but I wonder what he missed out on while being taught the syllabus, or while learning to read at the age of two and a half. I wonder if he has ever had time to play, in an undirected, 'non-educational', exploratory way, or to learn how to relate to his peers, since he has no siblings. And what will he do when his peers are all taking GCSEs and he has outstripped them academically? Will he follow others to Oxbridge at ten or start work in the City at thirteen? Where is the rush, and why is life already competitive for a five-year-old?

When our children were young, there was a local playgroup in the park, which doubled as a 'One O'clock Club' for carers and under-fives in the afternoons. The setting, equipment and leaders were excellent. Children were allowed time and space for free play without being subjected to the kind of formality in which all activities have to be structured, monitored and assessed in educational jargon. The mornings were spent playing in the sandpit, riding tricycles, painting, sticking, making feasts from playdough, listening to stories, or singing. Many local teenagers have golden memories of these times and so do their parents, because we knew that the children were unhurried, unpressurized, growing through their experiences to the stage when they were ready for formal schooling.

Time to be free

A Saturday afternoon visit to a large shopping centre a while ago reminded me that shopping is now our nation's number one leisure pursuit. But I am saddened to think of a generation of children growing up preferring retail therapy to a trip to the swings or a kick-around in the park. If our children are not allowed to be children, how much they are missing! Childhood is the time to enjoy simple, free, relaxing, time-wasting pursuits such as splashing in puddles, riding bikes, making tree houses or having water fights. Children are innately imaginative, but they will lose the ability to create their own games, dens, junk models or jewellery unless they have the time and space to do it. Childcare considerations clearly put pressure on families to arrange organized activities, but let us try not to programme every minute of their weekends or every day of their school holidays.

This 'free time' is also likely to be the time when children play with siblings, when the bedrock of shared memories is laid down, and when lasting friendships between brothers and sisters are sealed. It is important for children to play across age ranges, not always with their chronological peers. Siblings, stepsiblings, cousins and neighbours are all in a good position to do this. Games become far less competitive and more inclusive when those taking part are not all the same age, and this is more achievable at home than at school, where peer-group pressure often makes playing with younger children unacceptable.

One friend told me with relief how her eleven-year-old had chosen to spend a Saturday with her younger brothers, building a new outdoor run for their guinea pigs, rather than going shopping for clothes or make-up, as many of her pre-teen peers do at weekends. Another family took the opportunity of redecorating their living-room to hold a 'cavemen' party for their son's birthday. The guests, including his siblings, were provided with half-used pots of paint and asked to decorate the bare walls. A wonderful time was had by all, and the results were a vivid reminder of how creative and enthusiastic children are. Everyone was quite sad to have to cover the 'cave paintings' with wallpaper a few weeks later, when the redecoration was finally completed.

Again and again...

The power of repetition is very strong for children. I love hearing our children reminiscing, 'Do you remember when we used to...'. Anything that is enjoyed, and repeated, can acquire the status of a tradition and become a source of much satisfaction and security for children. Repeating familiar, everyday routines and actions somehow makes time slow down and helps everyone to enjoy simple 'childish' things like a walk in the park or feeding the ducks. Repeating activities with younger siblings benefits the older ones too: they are allowed to 'stay little' for a bit longer and revisit places they remember. Books and videos can have the same effect as older children share their favourites with younger brothers and sisters.

Holidays also build shared memories within the family, which strengthen and deepen all the relationships. Several parents commented on how well siblings got on when on holiday 'with no one else around to play with'. Returning to the same places on holiday or to stay with relatives builds the sense of time stretching both forwards and backwards, rather than everything being focused on 'now'. We've spent many family holidays on a Scottish island, which has a timeless quality for us because it holds both memories and hopes for the future. One of our children, when under pressure in the midst of school exams, told me that she just wished she was on 'our' beach outside the cottage, which, to her, epitomizes having time, space and freedom. Our son has already decided that he will take his children there, and is rather hoping that his parents might invest in a cottage to facilitate this dream. We admire his optimism...

Playing together

I heard a chance comment on the radio the other day which has stayed with me: 'You don't stop playing when you become a grown-up; you become a grown-up when you stop playing.' How true! If we allow our children to be children, they will also help us not to become 'boring grown-ups'. I remember, some years ago, having lunch with friends whose home always seemed gloriously hectic and happy as their three children were growing up. As we sat down for coffee, there was a lot of laughter and banging from the hall outside. Our host explained that it was only her husband teaching their youngest to abseil, down the banisters!

Children can tell the difference very quickly between adults who play and those who don't. Ours have always loved having guests for Sunday lunch, as long as they fall into the 'playing' category! Among the most popular was the friend who always had her nails painted when she came, spending ages discussing which colours they should be. Then there was the friend who never tired of playing card games and teaching us new ones, and another who discussed sport for hours with the children and took on all comers at table football. Playing together is very strengthening for families: it releases tensions, brings healing laughter and creates shared memories.

We have seen how important it is to give children time as they grow up. This is both time together in the family, so that their relationships with parents and siblings can develop, but also time to be children, protected from the prevailing culture that makes children grow up too quickly, 'forcing' them like spring flowers at Christmas, which bloom early but are dead before New Year.

Let's consider now the need for encouragement, which is the 'water' of the family.

POSITIVE INPUT

Our children desperately need encouragement as they grow up. All of us must have encountered adults who are so frightened of spoiling children by complimenting or praising them that they rarely say anything positive to them directly. I wonder how many of today's parents experienced this when they were young and are either repeating the process or going to the other extreme. Yet, as we have seen, each child needs *daily positive affirmation* as they begin to develop their own identity.

To encourage a child, simply and honestly, has the most amazing results. As a parent, I have seen this most clearly in our children's progress at school. The teachers who have helped them most and built up their confidence are not the ones who praised them lavishly (nor those who humiliated them for their shortcomings). They are the ones who built a strong relationship with the child, looked for their strengths and weaknesses and enabled the child to face up to them. For example, one of our children was discouraged in maths, and working very slowly in class for fear of making mistakes. A new teacher recognized this, but also recognized the child's potential and ability in mental arithmetic. Her encouragement, coupled with consistent teaching and high expectations, brought about a transformation in the work and the child.

There is a key difference between praise and encouragement. The first is to be used only on special occasions, rather like a dose of plant food, perhaps. The second is needed every day—simply, consistently and realistically applied, like watering a young plant. Children quickly see through praise when it is not merited. They may even dislike what seems to them 'over-the-top' praise. Encouragement, by contrast, is characterised by realism and honesty. To tell a child, 'Your handwriting is getting neater' is much more encouraging to them than to say, 'You're so clever.' A teenage girl would far rather hear,

'I like that new top: the colour suits you' than, 'You look beautiful', because she can believe and hold on to the first comment: the second is too big to handle. We have seen already how praise of one child in a family, if overheard by a sibling, will be interpreted as a negative comparison with them. Encouragement, by contrast, is less threatening to siblings as it refers to specific qualities or situations rather than broader value judgments. Of course we should and will praise our children when they overcome a fear, succeed at a task or test, win a competition, or reach a milestone. But let's reserve such praise for special occasions, so that the praise remains special too, and does not become devalued by overuse.

Practice makes perfect?

With daily practice, encouragement, like playing the violin, becomes both easier to do and easier to hear. We can encourage our children not just about the outward things, but the inward ones too. 'It was kind of you to offer your brother your new CD to listen to'; 'I noticed that you didn't shout back when she lost her temper with you. Well done.' Children who receive encouragement from their parents will gradually learn to encourage their siblings, to support and appreciate each other. It is a great joy for parents when one of their children asks their brother or sister, 'How was your day?' and then listens to the answer, or when they begin to compliment each other on how they look before they leave home for a party, or to express genuine pleasure in each other's successes.

When interests are shared, be they sport, music, cooking, or fashion, the opportunities for mutual encouragement multiply. I know of several families for whom sport takes them to a wide variety of locations to support each other, and the whole family goes whenever possible. When our children were at primary school, it was always interesting to see who came to watch the football team play. Often, older brothers and sisters would walk home a different way from their secondary school and 'just happen' to be there to watch the match, and younger siblings would be there with their parents, knowing that when their turn came, they could count on the same family support. It is clear on these occasions that not all the siblings present are interested in the sport in question, but they are there because they care about their brother or sister taking part, and they are learning to support each other on principle: 'if it matters to you, it matters to me.'

Don't force it!

Encouragement is, of course, the greatest antidote to discouragement. Many children feel discouraged, often in comparison to siblings and peers or as a result of the pressures upon them at home and school. I am a firm believer in what teachers used to call 'reading readiness'. This meant recognizing that each child learned to read at their own pace, and it was based on the conviction that, in the right environment, with plenty of encouragement and consistent teaching, the vast majority of children would learn to read well, *when they were ready*. National tests now dictate that all children should be at a certain level by the time they are seven years old, and those who aren't risk being labelled as failures. Teachers feel incredible pressure to 'get results', not only in reading but in all the core areas that are tested. I'm not against 'raising standards', or making sure that children progress, but I do fear for the many children who simply need a bit more time, help and positive input in order to learn. For them, being pushed, tested and compared with others only makes things more difficult.

At home, let's be careful not to add to the pressure that children are likely to face in school. Let's encourage them to achieve their potential, but not to compare themselves with others. Comparison with siblings is the source of much discouragement for children. One mother told me how devastated she felt when talking to a friend about her three sons, in the hearing of the youngest. She had said, 'James is the clever one, Paul is the artistic one...' then she paused, and heard her son complete the sentence, '... and George is the stupid one.'

Don't lose touch!

Sometimes words are inadequate to express our encouragement of our children. A look, a nod, a touch or a hug can say so much more. As our children get older, we need to be sensitive to them and not embarrass them, but we mustn't assume that they won't want or need physical touch from their parents. I clearly remember evenings as a teenager when I felt very confused and lonely, perhaps because my older siblings were no longer living at home. I would sit next to my mum on the sofa and she'd put her arm round me, and sometimes I'd cry too, if it had been a hard day for some reason. My mother didn't say anything that I remember, or ask me questions, but her physical presence was deeply reassuring and encouraging at a stage when I was particularly vulnerable.

We have considered time and encouragement, the 'light' and 'water' of the family growing medium. Finally, let's look at how unconditional love is the 'warmth' that is equally vital for our children as they grow.

ALL YOU NEED IS LOVE

In his fascinating book, *Christians in a Consumer Culture*, John Benton writes, 'The shift has been made from the inner life to the outward image.'[2]

This is the world in which today's children are growing up, and they have nothing else to compare it with, unless we provide that alternative in our families and churches. In a society that constantly gives the message that what we do or eat or wear is the key to who we are, we will have to work hard to counter this idea in our children with the truth that they are loved unconditionally, for who they are. We will look in Chapter 8 at how the church can use family principles to provide just such an alternative environment for people to relate to each other, to give and receive love. For the moment, let us focus on the child growing up and how the family can best maintain the warmth of unconditional love, rather than allowing cold blasts of judgment, resentment or criticism to damage our children's self-esteem as harshly as frost does a tender young plant.

I am always struck, when reading the stories of Old Testament leaders such as Moses, Joshua or Gideon, by how much reassurance they need. Every chapter contains the words, 'I am the Lord your God and I will be with you' or something similar. The reason, of course, is that God our heavenly Father knows the great need his children have for affirmation of their relationship with him and of his faithfulness to them. Similarly, the need to receive affirmation and unconditional love continues for each of us throughout our lives, and it begins very early.

A wise friend once advised me to say the immortal words 'I love you' to our new baby every evening as I put her to bed. She said this when I had been a parent for all of three months, and I followed her advice. As she said, 'If you begin now, you'll never stop; if you don't, you'll never start.' Although there are countless ways of demonstrating our love for our children without words, it is vital to tell them, simply and clearly, 'in words of one syllable', that we love them. It is also very helpful to use their names, as this makes our statement personal and powerful, linking our unconditional love to their individual identity at a deep level.

Terms and conditions

Our children need to know that we love them now, we have always loved them, and we always will. This is what unconditional love means. To understand this better, let's look for a moment at the opposite—love that is conditional. The word 'conditional' brings back memories for me of learning a foreign language at school, since this was the first time I encountered 'Grammar' with a capital G. The conditional tense of verbs was the one used to say, 'I could go to the park', 'I would like a drink' or 'I might come to the cinema'. All these tentative statements had hidden conditions attached to them: 'I could go to the park, if it stops raining'; 'I would like a drink, but I don't have any money on me'; 'I might come to the cinema, if I have nothing better to do'. They all implied an uncertainty because of outward circumstances or temporary feelings. Imagine saying to a child, 'I *might* love you if I wasn't so busy at work', or, 'I *could* love you if you stopped waking up every night.' Of course we wouldn't do it, but I wonder how often our children hear hidden conditions in what we say to them. For example, if we tell them we love them only when they have done something we approve of, the love they perceive will be conditional upon their behaviour or achievement.

A child of ten was very surprised, the night before a music exam, when her mother told her, 'I'll still love you just as much if you fail as if you pass!' She felt that she was taking the exam for her parents, and would be letting them down if she didn't make the grade. Her mother needed to explain that the result mattered to her only because she wanted her daughter to feel that she had succeeded, after months of practice, and that she'd be disappointed on her behalf if she failed, but not angry. She loved her, and passing the exam was not a condition of that love.

Nothing more, nothing less

A primary school teacher told me about a very able girl in his class who always completed her work quickly and well. Anxious to challenge and extend her, he would try to have a suitable response when she brought her work to show him. After some months in his class, he was looking at a finished piece of writing, saying, 'That's excellent, Sam...', when she interrupted him: 'BUT! There's always a but! No matter what I do, it's never quite good enough for you, is it?'

The girl, with the wisdom and insight of a child, was able to articulate how his conditional response made her feel. It was a moment of growth in their working relationship, and one that changed the teacher's approach both to his pupils and to his own children.

In our affirmation of children, let's keep it simple, not adding or subtracting anything, however positive our motives might be. We will need to bite back the added 'conditions'—throwaway phrases such as, 'Why can't you always behave like that?' or '... for a change'—which totally negate the positives we have expressed. Similarly, let us not subtract value from the child in any way. 'You did really well, but then your sister was always good at French too' means to the child that they're never going to match up to the older sibling. 'If you keep trying, you could be as good a footballer as your Uncle Bob' is likewise a recipe for discouragement, and totally demotivating.

To summarize, let us think back to John Benton's comment about inner life and outward image. Conditional love depends on what is outward and transitory; unconditional love depends on what is inward and life-giving. We learn how to give unconditional love only when we receive it ourselves, and the greatest source of such love is God. 'There is nothing we can do to make God love us more. There is nothing we can do to make God love us less,' as Philip Yancey expresses it.[3] The father's unconditional love, as expressed most clearly in Jesus' story of the prodigal son, has much to teach us, especially as it has at its heart two brothers whose relationship is far from close because neither of them feels secure in their father's love.

✥

BIBLE FOCUS: COMING HOME
THE PRODIGAL SON

Jesus told them another story: Once a man had two sons. The younger son said to his father, 'Give me my share of the property'. So the father divided his property between his sons.

Not long after that, the younger son packed up everything he owned and left for a foreign country, where he wasted all his money in wild living. He had spent everything, when a bad famine spread through that whole land. Soon he had nothing to eat.

He went to work for a man in that country, and the man sent him out to take care of his pigs. He would have been glad to eat what the pigs were eating, but no one gave him a thing.

Finally, he came to his senses and said, 'My father's workers have plenty to eat, and here I am, starving to death! I will go to my father and say to him, "Father, I have sinned against God in heaven and against you. I am no longer good enough to be called your son. Treat me like one of your workers."'

The younger son got up and started back to his father. But when he was still a long way off, his father saw him and felt sorry for him. He ran to his son and hugged and kissed him.

The son said, 'Father, I have sinned against God in heaven and against you. I am no longer good enough to be called your son.'

But his father said to the servants, 'Hurry and bring the best clothes and put them on him. Give him a ring for his finger and sandals for his feet. Get the best calf and prepare it, so we can eat and celebrate. This son of mine was dead, but has now come back to life. He was lost and has now been found.' And they began to celebrate.

The elder son had been out in the field. But when he came near the house, he heard the music and dancing. So he called one of the servants over and asked, 'What's going on here?'

The servant answered, 'Your brother has come home safe and sound, and your father ordered us to kill the best calf.' The elder brother got so angry that he would not even go into the house.

His father came out and begged him to go in. But he said to his father, 'For years I have worked for you like a slave and have always obeyed you. But you have never even given me a little goat, so that I could have a dinner with my friends. This other son of yours wasted your money on prostitutes. And now that he has come home, you ordered the best calf to be killed for a feast.'

His father replied, 'My son, you are always with me, and everything I have is yours. But we should be glad and celebrate! Your brother was dead, but he is now alive. He was lost, and has now been found.'

LUKE 15:11–32

Traditionally, this timeless story of Jesus has been known as 'the prodigal son'. The younger son has been blamed for foolishly wasting his inheritance, and the father's generosity in accepting him back has been praised as being beyond the bounds of human expectation. The role of the elder brother has remained as a rather dampening footnote to the story, sometimes omitted altogether. If mentioned, it is generally excused as being an understandable reaction to the younger son's unreasonable behaviour. Yet the elder brother is central to the story's impact, his response taking up the last eight verses—over a third of the story, in fact. The story is about two sons, and two brothers, about both parent–child and sibling relationships. We can easily read it and condemn the younger brother's actions without admitting that our own reactions often mirror those of the older brother.

To stay or go

It is the younger brother's idea to ask their father for his share of the property, but, in fact, both boys receive their share: the father does not withhold the older brother's inheritance. Both have the choice to stay at home or to leave. The older brother is not compelled to stay: it is even possible that his brother buys out his share so that he can realize the capital to take on his travels. Perhaps he feels duty-bound to continue managing the farm; probably he expects to be favourably compared with his brother, as the reliable and obedient one in the family. Maybe he rather envies his brother's daring in leaving; possibly he expects to receive more of his parents' attention now that there is no competition for it. But this is precisely where he goes wrong, because his father does not make comparisons between his two sons or 'gang up' with one against the other. He loves them both, equally and unconditionally. The older son finds this very hard to believe.

But, as Henri Nouwen writes, 'God does not measure out his love to his children according to how well they behave.' In his wonderful book based on Rembrandt's painting *The return of the prodigal son*, Nouwen describes God, the father in the story, thus:

The father's free and spontaneous response to his younger son's return does not involve any comparisons with his elder son. To the contrary, he ardently desires to make his elder son part of his joy. This is not easy for me to grasp. In a world that constantly compares people, ranking them as more or less intelligent, more or less attractive, more or less successful, it is not easy to really believe in a love that does not do the same...

Our God, who is both Father and Mother to us, does not compare. Never. Even though I know in my head that this is true, it is still very hard to accept it with my whole being.[4]

Jesus' story shows the father's unconditional love for both his sons, demonstrated in different ways and received very differently. The younger son's desperate decision to come home reveals that he still has some sense of his identity, that 'home' is still 'home' because of his father's love, even though he has now squandered his material share of the property. In Rembrandt's painting, the younger son, though ragged and exhausted, still wears his sword, the symbol of his sonship. His bitter experience of people who only love him conditionally, who use him and discard him, brings him to the realization that he is still his father's son, even though he no longer deserves to be called by that name. Thus he comes home humbled and grateful, expecting little, and is overwhelmed by the unconditional welcome he receives.

Anger and denial

The elder brother cannot stomach this display of unmerited love. The celebrations provoke in him an explosive, angry reaction, and he denies his relationship with his brother, calling him 'this son of yours'. Yet the father's unconditional love for his older son is evident in the way he goes out to meet him, to persuade him to come home and be reconciled with his brother. The father emphasizes that the sibling relationship must be healed, as well as the parent–child one. Verses 24 and 32 echo each other, with the significant difference that verse 24 refers to 'my son' and verse 32 to 'your brother': 'This son of mine (Your brother) was dead, but has now come back to life. He was lost and has now been found' (Luke 15:24, 32).

Only when both horizontal and vertical relationships are restored can the whole family celebrate.

Recently, a newspaper devoted its child health page to the problem of 'Why does my boy hit his brother?' The answer focused mainly on the elder brother's need to feel loved and valued, and to have time with his parent alone in which the parent could show their interest and involvement in his activities—time, in other words, for the older child to experience the parent's unconditional love, rather than making comparisons with his sibling. This is exactly what the father offers the older son in Jesus' story when he says, 'My son, you are always with me, and everything I have is yours' (Luke 15:31).

The story remains unresolved, because the father cannot force his older son to join the party, to believe that he is loved equally and unconditionally. He needs to be welcomed home just as much as his wayward brother, but will he see it?

To us, it is perhaps easier to forgive and welcome home someone who wants to be welcomed and forgiven. But God, represented by the father in the story, sees people's hearts and their true needs rather than the outward image they present. He loves the self-righteous elder brother as much as the repentant younger brother, however much we may think one is more deserving than the other. We are left, uncomfortably, not knowing whether the elder brother will let go of his resentment and receive his father's love for himself. As Jesus' story shows, it is very hard for us to believe that we are loved and valued in our families. The story also demonstrates that, until we do believe this, we will be unable to love and forgive our siblings.

❖

IN A NUTSHELL

In Chapter 5 we considered the family as the medium in which children grow.

Their basic needs are for time, encouragement and unconditional love. Each of these needs was looked at in practical detail, focusing on how parents can protect children from pressure to grow up too quickly. The key difference between praise and encouragement was noted, and the danger of allowing our love to become conditional. Jesus' story of the prodigal son underlines these needs, and the way sibling comparisons and resentment can disrupt family relationships.

GROWTH POINTS

- Think of your own childhood. How much time, encouragement and unconditional love did you experience? How have your experiences affected your relationships with children now?

- In your situation, what steps could you take to help children to 'be children' and not be pressurized to grow up too soon?

- What will 'unconditional love' mean in practice in a relationship that you find difficult?

- For further Bible study, read the story of the prodigal son again. Choose one character from the story (perhaps the one you identify with most) and write an account of what happened from their point of view. You could set it in a contemporary context if you wish. End with a brief summary, still in character, of how the events have affected you and your family. In a group, allow long enough to share what you have written by reading the accounts aloud, or swapping them, in pairs.

CLEARINGS

BECOMING WHO WE ARE

God leaves us free to be whatever we like. We can be ourselves or not, as we please. We are at liberty to be real, or to be unreal. We may wear now one mask, and now another, and never, if we so desire, appear with our own true face...

It is quite easy, it seems, to please everyone. But in the long run the cost and sorrow come very high. To work out our own identity in God... demands close attention to reality at every moment. Unless I desire this identity and work to find it with him and in him, the work will never be done.[5]

PRAYER

Lord, please work with me, and make me who I am. Amen

NOTES

1. Emily Drew, aged 10, from *Our poems and no messin'*, compiled by Margaret Cooling, Scripture Union, 1999, p. 32
2. John Benton, *Christians in a Consumer Culture*, Christian Focus Publications, 1999, p.168
3. Philip Yancey, *What's So Amazing About Grace?* Zondervan, 1997, p.70
4. Henri Nouwen, *The Return of the Prodigal Son*, Darton, Longman and Todd, 1994, pp. 105, 103
5. Thomas Merton, *A Selection of His Writings*, Templegate, 1990, p. 56

CHAPTER 6

OUT ON A LIMB: ENABLING CHILDREN TO DEVELOP THEIR IDENTITY AND INDEPENDENCE

A central feature... of parenting (is) the provision by both parents of a secure base from which a child or an adolescent can make sorties into the outside world and to which he can return knowing for sure that he will be welcomed when he gets there, nourished physically and emotionally, comforted if distressed, reassured if frightened.[1]

VITAL ATTACHMENTS

Mincer, chopper, blender, shredder, juicer, dough hook—these were the vital attachments that came with the shiny new electric mixer, the pride of my mother's kitchen in the 1960s. The more attachments it had, the further up the range the model was, or you could start with a basic mixer and add the 'vital attachments' as you went on. As long as the mixer was plugged into the right power source, it could be adapted to do all sorts of other things, apart from mixing sponge cakes.

The parallels to children are closer than we might think. I will refrain, however, from comparing older brothers with dough hooks, or little sisters with juicers. The real point is that a baby is born attached to its mother physically, through the vital link that provides it with food in the womb, and many mothers feel that they already have a relationship with their baby before it is born. In the early days after birth, the mother continues to be the source of everything the baby needs to thrive, physically and emotionally. The mixer is 'plugged in', we could say, unless there is a problem. This may be a health issue, for mother or baby, in which case hospitals will seek to maintain the contact as closely as possible. The other potential hindrance to the bonding or attachment process, and increasingly prevalent in our culture, is post-natal depression. In this case, the support network of family and friends is vital, both in preventing and arresting the cycle of illness.

As we saw earlier, in some cultures today (and in Britain in the past), mothers are 'confined' after birth and the family and community rally to keep the household running for about six weeks. There are aspects of this regime that many today would find restricting, but during this period the mother has time to recover her strength and to devote herself to the baby. Thus the priority of establishing the bond between mother and child is both recognized and facilitated.

If, for any reason, this mother–baby attachment cannot be continued outside the womb, another close bond must be substituted for it if the baby is to thrive. For, just as the extra attachments on the mixer will never work unless it is plugged into the power source, so a child will not be able to attach to other people, to build strong relationships, unless the first attachment is strong. That is why adoptive parents are happy to adopt children who have been in foster care since they were very tiny, as these children will have formed a strong attachment to at least one foster carer, and are more likely to bond with their new parents.

In the succeeding months and years, the growing child will form other attachments, to include both parents, siblings, grandparents and others in the wider circle of family and friends. These relationships will help to determine and define the child's sense of his or her own identity. There is another process, however, which must also take place.

LETTING GO

We were on holiday in Bath, sitting near the Abbey eating ice-creams. Our daughter, not quite two years of age, was clutching her lolly wrapper, and spotted a large bin across the square. Taking my wrapper in the other hand, she marched boldly to the bin, deposited both, then turned and grinned triumphantly at me before walking back to our bench on her own. That was the first time I remember any of our children going somewhere public on their own— a journey of ten metres, taking about a minute there and back. Yet for both of us, it was a major achievement, a sign of her growing confidence and an endorsement of the trust between us. A large part of me did not want to let her go on her own, but I'm glad I bit my tongue and didn't stop her.

I thought back to that incident as I read the advice given in a teen parenting course: 'Never do for teenagers anything which they can do for themselves.' A lot of 'letting go' by parents is necessary in the years between toddler and teen. Parents need wisdom to recognize and take the opportunities to do this as they arise. Letting go is a vital process, and needs to be done gently and gradually, from birth onwards—in fact, from the moment the umbilical cord is cut. This needs to go hand in hand with the attachment process that we have already considered.

Healthy families—healthy children

We want our families to be healthy, not only for the sake of the family unit, but so that each individual within it will grow into a mature adult, able to support and potentially parent or care for others. For Christians, this is closely linked to the hope that our children will also find security and identity in their relationship with God, and within the wider context of a church 'family'. Slowly and steadily, children begin to go 'out on a limb', but they desperately need to stay attached to the trunk, the family base, as they take these first steps of independence and self-discovery. Identity is also tested and strengthened through the key points that each child faces as they grow up. We will discover that development varies for children in different family positions, and we will consider what impact this position has, for example, on the oldest, only child or twin.

Key points

A family is not static and the most successful ones are the most adaptable, ready to grow and change and accommodate the changing relationships within it.[2]

As we saw in Chapter 2, there are a number of key points in the life of every family, at which the changes children experience mark huge leaps forward. The first man on the moon, Neil Armstrong, famously took 'one small step for man, one giant leap for mankind'. Conversely, our children take 'small steps' in terms of following a well-trodden path, but for each individual they are 'giant leaps'. These key points fall into two groups or categories—those we can anticipate, which are common to nearly all children, and those that apply particularly to individual family circumstances.

In the first category, key points are mostly to do with education and physical development—starting nursery, primary school, and then secondary school; leaving school; starting college or work; and, eventually, leaving home. Then there's learning to crawl, walk, talk, read, ride a bike and swim. Adolescence brings a whole new set of milestones—the first period for girls, boys' voices breaking, first boyfriend or girlfriend, moving from pocket money to an allowance, earning money for the first time, independent social activities without parents, and learning to drive.

In the second category come key points which not all children experience, and which we may be less able to predict, although in some cases we can prepare our children for them. These points mainly involve change and loss, and include illness or disability; the death of a pet, a family member or friend; moving house or school; the loss of a friend who moves; the birth of siblings; parents' separation, divorce or remarriage; new stepbrothers and sisters; and new family structures.

In this chapter we will consider the key points in children's development up to adolescence and how the processes of attachment and letting go work together at these times. We will move through these events chronologically, and also bear in mind the differences that family position makes. For example, parents experience their children's learning to walk very differently depending on whether it is the first child or subsequent children doing so, although it is equally momentous for each individual child.

UNDER FIVES: FIRST STEPS AND GIANT LEAPS

We have already seen how important it is that babies are 'attached' and, as children grow, they continue to need these bonds. For the first two years of life, they will form bonds mainly with adults; after that, sibling relationships and those with peers begin to be established. The first significant change for both parents and children to negotiate is when babies become toddlers. Many parents feel unprepared for and unsettled by their children's newfound independence as they learn to walk and talk. It was much less stressful when they merely sat and gurgled, or even cried. In fact, it can seem much easier to love a baby than a toddler, and parents may experience guilt at the frustration and anger their toddler provokes in them. Advice and encouragement from family, friends or parenting groups can really help at this stage, for the parents are also finding their way through uncharted waters.

Toddlers need consistent reassurance and love, in order to have the confidence to take on all the new challenges that are before them. What is going on for them at this time? If we could get inside a toddler's head, we might find them feeling lost and discouraged by the change in how they are treated—there are more commands, restrictions and nagging, fewer spontaneous hugs and smiles. What they may assume is that they now need to earn their parents' approval. All this change may also be exacerbated by a new baby, cooed over and cuddled by family and friends, who is receiving all the 'undeserved' positive attention that the toddler is missing. So how do we stay positive and strengthen the attachments for a toddler? Many of the ways we have considered in earlier chapters help here: one-to-one time and attention, having fun together, repetition of familiar, enjoyed routines, and as many ways as possible of reinforcing the special bond between parent and child. This is often best done through little things—a secret wink or smile across a room, a small treat that shows you have remembered a particular preference they've expressed, or a request to help which makes them feel trusted and valued.

If there is a baby in the family, it is important to build in activities which are clearly for the toddler's benefit, not the baby's. The helpers at our church toddler group spend a lot of time holding babies (and loving the chance to do so), so that parents and carers can focus on their older child, make a model with them, read them a story or help them paint, print or stick without interruption. This positive input will gradually foster confidence and security, enabling the child to become more independent and to make new attachments with other adults and children. A newspaper article expressed this well:

Many parents make the mistake of confusing an attached child with a clinging child, which is quite wrong. Attached means loved... You don't create independent children by pushing them to stand on their own two feet—the most independent and confident children are those who feel most securely attached to their parents.[3]

Apron strings

Let's look now at how the 'letting go' process affects babies and toddlers. It may seem strange to think of letting go of a baby, yet I believe that it is important for both parent and child. If the baby is breastfed, it may be important for the mother occasionally to allow someone else to feed the baby from a bottle. This not only has huge practical benefits, like giving the mother a break, but it also enables other people, such as the baby's father or older siblings, to bond with the infant and enjoy the closeness of the experience. Similarly, the earlier parents allow other people to take care of their child for short periods, the better. A baby of a few months old is often happy to be left with a grandparent or friend so that the parent can have a haircut or go Christmas shopping, or in a crèche so that they can attend a church service. But if the baby first experiences 'being left' at a later stage, perhaps when the pressure is on as maternity leave ends, it will be much harder for both parent and child. 'Do it before you need to' is good advice for this, all the way through. If we can anticipate the changes that face our children, we can prepare for them gently and gradually.

With toddlers, we need to be 'letting go', but within boundaries set for their safety, which also teach them what is and is not acceptable behaviour. Young children love to explore and experiment, and much can be done to provide them with safe and appropriate opportunities to do this. Bathtime can be the start of scientific discovery with plastic cups, bottles and funnels, but allow enough time and don't put precious ornaments or expensive carpet in the bathroom. A muddy walk can be a great shared adventure, so don old clothes and wellies all round; even take a bin bag and a change of clothes! Forethought and preparation are the keys to letting our children explore and experiment, and also to feeling in control enough to be firm and clear about what children can and can't do.

Same again?

We have thought mainly about the first toddler in a family. The experience of subsequent children as toddlers will be different, especially because it will feature their siblings very prominently. One little boy was heard to say his older sister's name, some weeks before he ever said 'Dada' or 'Mama', as toddlers are initially supposed to. Younger children in a family have at least one ready-made playmate, who will (you hope) be waiting eagerly for them to become mobile and learn how to kick a football or play games. They enter into a family unit which is already established, rather than still emerging. One mother describes her five children as a 'gang', the older ones organizing play activities for the younger ones; and younger toddlers have the benefit of the older ones' help and attention, as well as their toys and games.

When younger siblings are toddlers, parents will often be focusing on the oldest, who may be starting school and embarking on the next phase of life, but we need to be sure the younger ones do not miss out on activities that the older ones have grown out of. In addition, parents usually feel much more relaxed with changes that mark key points when they reach them second or third time around, but it is still a very big step for the child concerned. For instance, by the time the second child goes to playgroup or nursery, the parents are well used to their role. The child may also have been there often, to collect or drop off a sibling, but we must not underestimate the experience for them, particularly if big brother or sister has now moved on. In families with more than two children, the first and last child's milestones will also be key points for their parents, yet they are also just as significant for the middle children in the family.

One is one

A family with one child is also very much a family, although much in our media seems to imply that one child is not enough to be a 'proper' family. Let us be careful not to fall into this danger, particularly since parents of only children may have chosen this arrangement, or they may be unable to have more children and may feel this keenly. Certainly the parent–child relationships in a family of three (or two if there is a lone parent) will be different from those in larger families. One mother of an only child expressed it thus, when talking about choices for her daughter's education: 'We're putting all our eggs in one basket. We don't want to get it wrong!' This same mother was wise enough to see the danger of putting too much pressure on her child, and of the mother–child bond becoming too intense, so the decisions that she made with their child were informed by this awareness. Fifteen years later, they enjoy healthy and close relationships now that she is an adult. Another parent of an only child spoke of the challenge for parents:

Raising an only child is not easy because they have no live-in companions and no competition. It is difficult to convey the idea of sharing and showing consideration for others… I have tried to compensate for my daughter's lack of siblings by making her friends welcome and encouraging her in activities involving other young people.

A father who was an only child had become very self-sufficient when he was small, playing for hours by himself. Later, as a teenager, he resisted all attempts by parents to get him 'out'. He recognized how this early experience still influenced him as an adult, in a need to spend time on his own and to have one close friend rather than a larger group. There will be particular pressures on parents of only children, and on the children themselves. One of these is the 'second baby' stage, when friends who have had their first children around the same time become pregnant again. This can be very painful for a mother or father who would like another child but is unable to have one. Toddlers in these circumstances become very interested in babies, and may demand a baby of their own and be jealous of friends who have younger siblings.

Double act

We're twins. I'm Ruby. She's Garnet. We're identical. There's very few people who can tell us apart. Well, until we start talking. I tend to go on and on. Garnet is much quieter.[4]

Families with twins face special opportunities and challenges. Parents' support groups provide much friendship, advice and practical help. The need for this help is tremendous in the early years especially, when there is twice as much washing, feeding and nappy-changing to be done. The effect on older children in the family is also significant, as so much of parents' time and energy is devoted to the babies. Siblings are also likely to feel excluded from and threatened by the close bond that exists between twins. A further factor is that the introduction of IVF has made multiple birth a much more common occurrence, and in Britain the number of triplets born has also risen, from 105 sets in 1985 to 285 sets in 2000.

For such children, the issue of developing identity and independence is especially important. Being a twin (or triplet) is central to a person's identity throughout their life. Because, in our mobile society, we often know one twin or triplet without knowing their sibling(s), this information may not be common knowledge. Interestingly, as I spoke to adults about their childhood, one of the first things that several chose to tell me was that they were twins. This fact is very close to the heart of 'who I am', even for adults with children of their own.

One woman vividly remembers starting school without her twin sister, who was ill on the crucial first day. Having reached every other milestone so far with her sister at her side, this proved a traumatic experience for the child, to the bemusement of the adults present. It is important to recognize that the bond between twins may be as strong as that between parent and child. In *Double Act*, Jaqueline Wilson's wonderful children's novel about twins, the sibling bond is especially strong because the twins' mother has died. Their 'double act' is tested as the family changes and as they each seek to establish their own identity, both with and without each other. Through this process, the 'love–hate' dynamic of siblings is very clear, as they first go to extreme lengths in trying to be different from each other, then swear to be best friends for ever. What the book makes clear is that the twins need individual attention, from their father, grandmother and stepmother, as they experience this rollercoaster of emotions. Also, their happiness as individuals is directly related to the health of their relationship with each other.

OFF TO SCHOOL: A TASTE OF INDEPENDENCE

At nursery, children are usually taken into the classroom, helped to hang up their coats and handed over to the teacher. When they start 'big' school, we are likely to leave them at the door to hang up their own coats and join their class. As juniors, we leave them in the playground or drop them at the school gate, and eventually we stop taking them to school altogether. One head teacher struck fear into the hearts of 'new' parents every September with her insistence that they should leave their children at the door and not come into school with them. She would patrol the cloakroom and evict any parent who dared to enter. Her methods were harsh, but the principle was right. By the age of five, the vast majority of children are ready and able to go into school on their own, and they need to be allowed to do so by their parents. The elastic of the parent–child bond is stretched further and further as the child becomes more independent. But we never let go of it altogether, even if we come into school less and less often and they travel to and from school independently. This is just one example of the 'attachment' and 'letting go' that need to happen at this stage.

Staying attached as children start school largely involves listening and remembering. First of all, listening is vital. A parent asked her children when they felt really listened to. They said, 'When you stop what you're doing and look at us.' We can think we are listening as we peel potatoes, empty the washing machine or tidy up, but our children will not feel really listened to unless we stop and focus on them exclusively. Changing family timetables and work routines mean that we have to keep reassessing when we can do this, but it needs to be a high priority or our children will stop talking to us. Just a few minutes is often enough to keep the communication going, but there will be times when we have to 'drop everything' to listen, even if it means not attending a meeting, or doing the ironing at midnight. Listening also helps us to discover what really matters to our children, which school subjects (and teachers) they love and hate, how they like to spend their break times, and who their friends are. We'll return to friends later as they become increasingly important in our children's worlds.

Secondly, remembering what our children tell us is crucial. This seems to get harder as they and we get older, but asking them specific questions about things they've mentioned is a key way to show that we care. It's much easier to fling out a random 'How was school?' than to remember to ask, 'How did your singing practice/spelling test/science experiment go?' But the general question is likely to get a general reply: 'Fine/OK/Boring', whereas the second usually elicits a much fuller reply and is a signal to them that we are willing to listen. I now jot things my children tell me in my diary so that I don't forget them. Similarly, as we remember their preferences, we help their sense of their own identity to develop—their distinctiveness, their sense of 'who they are'.

So, staying attached involves listening and remembering, both of which build up the child's self-esteem. At the same time, we continue to let our children go, and the most obvious area in which we do this is in their friendships.

Making friends

In the pre-school years, most children's friendships are determined by adults: they play with cousins, neighbours or other children introduced to them by their parents or carers. Only at playgroup or nursery will they come into contact with other children not 'chosen' by their parents, directly or indirectly, although parents may choose a nursery, and later a school, partly on the basis of the other children who are there. Children who grow up in a church community may form strong friendships which begin through their parents but go on to function independently of the adults. When this happens, it is very positive for both families as all the relationships are enhanced.

As children start school, they also start to make friends without their parents, and this is one of the hardest things to adjust to as they get older. As they start inviting friends to tea, parents soon work out which children they hope will be long-term friends.

Talking with other parents at this stage, we decided that we should be positive about all our children's friends, encourage them to bring friends home and not try to manipulate their choices, much as we might wish to. It is a big step for children to introduce their friends to us, and we must not betray their trust or embarrass them; yet we need also to be consistent in the way we do things, so that the home environment remains stable. If we usually say grace before meals, we still do so, even if this is a strange experience for friends. If there are older or younger brothers and sisters, all the children will have tea together, so that the friend is included in the whole family. A mother of four comments on the challenge of such situations: 'Group dynamics change noticeably when children's friends come, often causing friction if there is a clash of interests... siblings vie for control of the situation!'

Sometimes, however, it is a friend's attitude to their siblings that helps our children to decide about the future prospects of the friendship. For example, when Kelly has her friend Sarah to tea, Sarah talks to Kelly's little brother Luke at tea-time and doesn't laugh at him when he spills his drink. But when Kelly's friend Mandy comes to tea, she calls Luke names and makes fun of him for being messy. So is Kelly more likely to feel relaxed with Sarah or with Mandy? And who is likely to be a better friend? Over time, children work out who they feel most at ease with at home, who 'fits in' to their lives because of common interests and values, and who is a friend with whom they can 'be themselves'.

The other side of friendships is that our children visit a wider range of families, and encounter home environments that are very different from their own. This is important for them, as they realize for the first time that not all families are like their own. It is enriching to see different ways of doing things, but it will also be challenging and they will come home with many questions: 'Why can't we have satellite television like Joe's family?' 'Why does Kuldip's granny live with them?' 'Why isn't Danny's dad ever there?' 'Why doesn't Michelle's family live in a flat/house like ours?' As we respond to these questions, listen to our children and remember what they tell us, we can help them to begin to make sense of their world, with all the diversity and inequality that it contains. They will also begin to see where they fit into it, and what makes them and their family unique.

Finally, a word of reassurance about friendships, and it takes us back again to the attachment process: 'Children socialize more easily if they know you (parents) feel good about them. Children who cannot be sure they are adored at home are far more likely to behave aggressively towards their schoolfriends.'[5]

Safe places

At this stage, attachments to adults other than parents will also be very important. Within the family, grandparents, aunts and uncles can form close and trusting relationships with children, which affirm them and give them confidence. These family members may invite the child to stay away from home, without parents, which can be a huge step towards independence, and introduce the child to people, places and life patterns which are different from those at home. The early years are the best time to forge these links: children never forget the unconditional love of a grandparent or great-grandparent, which may be there for only a few years before the older person dies. To pass on this closeness through the generations is a very precious thing. Shortly after the death of her own mother, a woman was hugely comforted to hear her young daughter tell a friend at church how well she felt she had known her granny, and how close they had been. In addition, getting to know older relatives well will help the children to relate to older people in the wider community. Fergal Keane writes movingly about his visits to his grandmother as a child:

My memories are of a happy place where comfort and reassurance were always at hand. Because of my father's alcoholism, my own home environment was neither happy nor secure. Taking the train to Cork and St Declans and the warm arms of my grandmother seemed to me an annual deliverance.[6]

We have seen how other adults can both be strong 'attachments' for our children, and also help the 'letting go' process as they get older. For many people, however, the wider family is not there to offer this support. Many families live at great distances from each other, or are separated because of family tensions or breakdown. We need people nearby—friends in the local community or church—with whom our children can form safe, trusting relationships as they 'go out on a limb' growing up.

We were fortunate to have friends living round the corner from us when our children were small. Their sons, who were older, learned about babysitting at our house, knowing that their parents were only five minutes away in an emergency. As our children got older, we'd send them round the corner on 'errands' to our friends, to borrow missing ingredients when cooking, to deliver or collect messages and so on. It was a 'safe' excursion, with a warm reception at the other end, and only one road to cross. The children's confidence grew, and they looked on this family as part of our wider family. Although we no longer live nearby, these relationships continue to be the source of support and empathy for all concerned, as they have been over the years, meeting crises together, celebrating each other's milestones, and watching our children grow into independent adults.

We need each other! Primarily the relationships in the family, but also those in the extended family and local church or community, are the launchpad for children as they grow up. Let us value them as this parent did, when he wrote to thank the leaders of a Christian holiday that his two children had enjoyed:

I appreciate the importance of the positive role modelling that my children have experienced from adults other than their parents sharing their own faith and encouraging and affirming them. I am sure that the experiences and memories will have had a positive influence on them as they mature physically, emotionally and spiritually.[7]

It is unrealistic, however, to expect all the influences on our children as they grow up to be positive. In the following pages, we will consider the tempestuous relationships in the Bible between King Saul, his son Jonathan and David, the shepherd boy who became king in Saul's place.

✥

BIBLE FOCUS: DAVID
LIVING THE COVENANT

Jesse was a farmer in Bethlehem in Judah, with eight sons, of whom David was the youngest. The three oldest were on military service in the army of King Saul, who was leading Israel against the neighbouring Ammonites and Philistines. Saul's campaigns were generally successful, but this time they had reached a stalemate because of a huge Philistine warrior called Goliath. Well, many of us know what happens next. But it is not quite as simple as we may remember.

David regularly delivers supplies from home to his brothers at the army camp, and one day he arrives in time to see the armies lining up to fight, then hears Goliath's challenge to the Israelites. From raw recruits to royal commander, they are all totally paralysed by fear— they run away. David is incensed by this performance: 'Who does that worthless Philistine think he is? He's making fun of the army of the living God!' (1 Samuel 17:26).

David makes enquiries among the soldiers, despite being told off by his brother Eliab for getting in the way. Eliab is angry, or perhaps embarrassed, that David sees the Israelite army suffering its daily humiliation. He wants to keep him in his place:

'What are you doing here, anyway? Who's taking care of that little flock of sheep out in the desert? You spoilt brat! You came here just to watch the fighting, didn't you?' (1 Samuel 17:28). But word of the impertinent boy reaches Saul, who asks to see him. With youthful honesty and naïvety, David tells Saul, 'This Philistine shouldn't turn us into cowards. I'll go out and fight him myself!' (1 Samuel 17:32).

David's legendary determination and courage are motivated by his concern for the whole people of Israel, as represented by its army. He is not bothered that Saul has offered his daughter's hand in marriage as a reward to anyone who will fight Goliath. He is not interested in protecting himself with Saul's own armour. He simply cannot stand by and allow God's people to be incapacitated by the outward show of strength and tough tactics of a bully. With the carelessness, or confidence, born of a right sense of his own worth, he stands up to Goliath.

Knowing me, knowing you

The much-loved story of David's victory over Goliath demonstrates two key characteristics of the man who went on to be Israel's greatest king. David knew God and he knew himself. These two relational strengths were crucial throughout David's life. We have further insight into David through the Psalms, which complement the stories of his life in the Bible books of 1 and 2 Samuel and 1 Chronicles. Many of his psalms demonstrate both self-knowledge, leading to repentance, and a certainty that God is powerful, just and merciful: 'I am poor and needy, but you, the Lord God, care about me. You are the one who saves me. Please hurry and help!' (Psalm 70:5).

David's faith in God is strong, nurtured through his years of shepherding, proven in his courage to face Goliath. His relationship with God is a deep and trusting friendship, and it is the foundation of David's life. It is also a covenant relationship, for David knows that the commitment is mutual: 'You, Lord, are all I want! You are my choice, and you keep me safe... I am your chosen one. You won't leave me in the grave or let my body decay' (Psalm 16:5, 10).

David has claimed as his own the covenant between God and Israel. This faith equips him not only to lead the nation against other nations, but also to call his people to follow God: 'Our Lord, you are the friend of your worshippers, and you make an agreement with all of us' (Psalm 25:14).

David understands covenant relationships, which are built on mutual trust and loyalty. This does not stop him from breaking such trust himself, but he knows the severity of such actions; he understands that honesty and integrity really matter. He also experiences betrayal from those whom he trusts, and knows what it is to trust God when everyone else has deserted him (see Psalms 15, 26 and 51).

In the years that follow the conquest of Goliath, David's life is far from plain sailing. He has already been anointed by Samuel as the next king of Israel. But it looks a totally impossible promise: Saul is very much alive and has three sons to succeed him. Added to that, David's brothers have turned against him, perhaps as a result of being overlooked by Samuel. Not unlike Joseph's brothers, they are jealous of David, as Eliab's reaction to him at the army camp showed. David is quite a lonely figure, in human terms, although he does have a strong sense of his family and national identity, since he tells Saul, 'I am David the son of Jesse, a loyal Israelite from Bethlehem' (1 Samuel 17:58).

God uses David's natural attributes, as soldier and musician, to bring him into Saul's court. David leaves his home and family at Saul's command and finds himself in the best possible place to learn about the reality of kingship. Unwittingly, Saul 'adopts' him into the royal family, where David forms a strong friendship with Saul's oldest son Jonathan, so that they become like brothers. When Native Americans formed such friendships, they cut their arms and mingled their blood to signify their mutual loyalty as 'blood brothers'.

This God-given friendship is remarkable because David knows that he will succeed Saul, and will, in fact, usurp the throne from Jonathan. But the strength of their covenant is such that even when Jonathan recognizes that David will be king in his place, he is able to accept it and support him. Not only that, but when Saul becomes obsessed with his envy of David, it is Jonathan who enables his friend to escape and protects him from his father's schemes to murder him. Chapters 18—24 of 1 Samuel make a good read!

Promise of the covenant

The relationship between David and Jonathan is highly significant in God's plan, therefore, for David and for Israel. Their covenant breaks the power of Saul's jealousy and ensures peace for Israel, because it removes the threat of revenge and hatred between their families in the future: 'Jonathan said, "Take care of yourself. And remember, we have each asked the Lord to watch and make sure that we and our descendants keep our promise for ever"' (1 Samuel 20:42).

This promise echoes David's relationship with God, which is itself a sign of the relationship between God and Israel—a covenant relationship.

A speaker at a Christian conference said this: 'Our society is in freefall as far as relationships are concerned. The answer to brokenness is belonging. The understanding of belonging that we all need is found in the Bible: and the Bible's teaching on belonging is the Covenant.'[8]

In the life of David we see a very human example of how covenant is lived out, in his relationship with God, with himself, and with others. It is encouraging to us because David makes mistakes and feels that he is 'a worm' (Psalm 22:6); it is inspiring because he looks beyond his problems to God's faithfulness and fairness (Psalm 36:5–6). As we saw earlier, he knows himself, but he also knows God. David suffers rejection by his family and betrayal by friends (Psalm 55:12–14), yet still trusts God. His friendship with Jonathan, although it ends tragically, plays a key part in God's plan for his people.

Throughout history, God has used friendships that cross barriers of self-interest to break the power of hatred. God still uses such covenant friendship today. The consequences may, or may not, be of national significance, but they will bring transformation to families, churches and communities.

❖

IN A NUTSHELL

In this chapter we have studied the processes of attachment and letting go, their importance and factors that help or hinder them.

Key points in children's development were outlined, and stages from birth to primary school discussed. The influence of family position was noted, and the particular needs and experiences of twins. Early friendships and 'safe places' outside the home can provide caring and affirming relationships as children grow in independence. Finally, the life of David illustrated the importance of covenant relationships.

GROWTH POINTS

- Consider the particular pressures that new parents face. What is the most effective support and help to offer them? Who can best offer this help, and what is the role of the local church here?

- Do you agree that 'attachment' and 'letting go' are equally important as we bring up children? What was your experience of these processes in your own childhood? Which do you find easier in your dealings with children, and how could you find a better balance between the two?

- Look again at the key points listed on page 107. Which are you encountering at the moment in the lives of the children you know? How can you adapt to accommodate the changes in relationships? (In a group, focus on one or two key points that affect a majority of group members.)

- For further Bible study, choose one of these Psalms to read: 15, 25 or 26. (In a group, you could break into twos or threes and read one psalm each.) What insights do you find here into David's relationship with God, with himself and with others?

  David's friendship with Jonathan mirrored his own relation-ship with God. For Christians, how can friendship with God strengthen our human friendships?

CLEARINGS

A WISH FOR MY CHILDREN

On this doorstep I stand
year after year
and watch you leaving

and think: May you not
skin your knees. May you not

catch your fingers
in car doors. May
your hearts not break.

May tide and weather
wait for your coming

and may you grow strong
to break
all webs of my weaving.[9]

PRAYER

God our parent,
Teach us how to love our children
As you love us:
To hold them tight
In the bonds of love
And to let them go
As we entrust them to you.
Amen

NOTES

1. John Bowlby, *A Secure Base: Clinical Applications of Attachment Theory*, Routledge, 1988, p.11
2. Miranda Ingram, 'The key to a happy family', *The Times*, 7 September 2000
3. Miranda Ingram, 'The key to a happy family'
4. Jacqueline Wilson, *Double Act*, Corgi Yearling, 1996, p. 1
5. Miranda Ingram, 'The key to a happy family'
6. Fergal Keane, *Letter to Daniel*, BBC, 1998, p. 16
7. *@SU*, Scripture Union Scotland, June 2002
8. Mike Breen, 'The Covenant', New Wine Conference, August 2000
9. Evangeline Paterson, from *Lucifer, with Angels*, Dedalus Press, Dublin

CHAPTER 7

NEW HORIZONS: ADOLESCENCE AND TEENAGERS, HUMAN MATURITY AND RELATIONSHIPS

Question

*Who else could ever
Fit into this head
Look through these holes
And see this particular view?*[1]

Through primary school, the process of individual development usually continues steadily, but the pace of change accelerates when children start secondary school. For girls, this is likely also to coincide with puberty; for boys, the physical changes most often kick in a year or two later.

GROWING UP: THE CHALLENGES OF ADOLESCENCE

Friendships and peer groups become the most significant factors for children as they reach adolescence. The attachments to parents, wider family and other adults are still crucial, however. Although their influence may seem to diminish at this time, they remain as a secure base through the turbulent teenage years. Adults other than parents may be a 'safe place' for teenagers to talk through problems, to 'be themselves' at times when life in the family is hard going.

Youth leaders, coaches, teachers, school counsellors and advisers may all take on this 'mentoring' role. For all adults in this position of trust with a teenager, much of what has already been suggested continues to apply. Staying attached still involves listening and remembering, making time to find out what is going on in the young person's life, what really matters to them.

Teenagers live in the present, and have a tendency to share their plans, and ask for our consent to them, as they are walking out of the door. They are not aware of the wider picture—of how their actions affect the rest of the family—unless we help them, indeed train them, to be so. It is well worth establishing a habit of planning together—asking a teenage son or daughter in advance to be around for family occasions, and not assuming that their time is at our disposal. This becomes especially important when teenagers reach the age at which they can 'babysit' for their own siblings or others. Payment arrangements need to be discussed and agreed, and it is helpful for parents to 'book' their son or daughter in advance, rather than assuming that they will be at home whenever needed. This approach gives teenagers an increased sense of value, which in turn encourages them to be more responsible.

Good communication is the hallmark of healthy families as the children reach adolescence. It is hard to maintain, however, once teenagers are out of the home more often and when their moods and hormones take them, and the rest of the family, on an emotional rollercoaster. Yet parents need to stay in touch—not to give up the affectionate rituals of a goodnight kiss, or prayers at bedtime, or a hug as they go off to school. And we need to be informed about what they are doing, not just for their safety, but to build the relationship of trust into its next phase. Boundaries and guidelines need to be discussed, agreed and applied. It is no good agreeing a time for children to be home and then ignoring their late arrival. On the other hand, it is no good setting a time to meet our children from a social activity and then being late ourselves. This is hard work, but an excellent investment for future relationships.

Study after study attests that healthy, happy and self-reliant adolescents and young adults are the products of stable homes in which both parents give a great deal of time and attention to the children.[2]

Question time

Many parents of teenagers feel reluctant to ask their children questions, for fear of 'prying'. But if we do not do so, the message we give is that we don't care. It all depends on how we ask. Closed, interrogative questions do not help; they merely emphasize the gap in viewpoint between the adult and the teenager. We need to ask open and affirmative questions, which require more than a monosyllabic answer and which allow the teenager to express their feelings and opinions. 'Tell me about the party?' is a better line than 'Who's going to the party?' Try 'How do you think we should spend Christmas this year?' rather than 'Why don't you want to go to Auntie Flo's on Boxing Day?' The aim is to affirm, not to threaten; to care, not to criticize.

Teenagers are faced with a mass of choices and, consequently, decisions at an ever earlier stage in their lives. They will have the confidence to make good choices for themselves only if they feel good about themselves and sure about the love of those to whom they are 'attached'. This will also be the critical factor when problems arise, friendships disintegrate, a young heart is broken, or boundaries are pushed too far. The son who is arrested as a teenager survives and learns from the experience, not because his parents lecture him but because they love him, stand by him and go with him to court. The daughter who becomes pregnant at fifteen comes through and copes when her parents listen, understand and love her, putting aside their disappointment and anger in order to help her make good choices about her future. As parents stand alongside their children, they will enable them to face problems with maturity, which is a crucial part of real life. 'A mature child, or for that matter a mature adult, accepts reality, with its frustrations, limitations, and, at times, profound disappointments, with equanimity—rather than fighting it with fury.'[3]

In a radio interview, a woman who had been in prison in Thailand for several years after committing drug-related offences spoke movingly of her parents' refusal to give up on her. They ignored her pleas to forget her and get on with their lives, and never gave up hope of her release. Now free, the woman says simply, 'I am sincerely blessed to have such parents.'

Jump... or be pushed!

In the last chapter I mentioned the advice, 'Never do for teenagers anything that they can do for themselves.' This is a sound principle, but raises the problem that parents and teenagers will often disagree about what they can do for themselves. Parents are likely to think that their sons and daughters can keep their rooms tidy, wash up, or cook meals for themselves. Teenagers may be reluctant to do any of these, but feel that they can stay out late, find their own way home from parties, and keep on top of all their schoolwork. Good communication is vital, again, in order to agree, rather than living in an atmosphere of tension and confrontation. This parent of teenagers advocates 'family conferences', which may involve as few as two or, in their case, up to six family members: 'We have on occasions had family conferences about specific issues—not just problems—and discussions together have helped strengthen relationships.'

In some cases, it may not be the teenagers who are pushing the boundaries. Not all teenagers 'rebel', and many tiptoe cautiously through the minefield of adolescence, needing reassurance and encouragement to try new things and make new friends. What happens at home is very important: it will either give teenagers confidence or tend to make them feel inadequate. We can build up their self-esteem by giving them responsibility in the family, not doing everything for them, and by treating them with respect as emerging adults rather than children. We need to have realistic expectations—neither pressurizing our teenagers to grow up too soon, nor stopping them from moving out into activities, friendships and eventually an identity that is independent.

After you...

What about the child's position in the family at this stage? Siblings watch each other closely—the younger ones to see what is coming next, the older ones to check that parents are being fair. This usually gives the younger child an advantage in the teenage years. Major changes face parents at this stage, and they are more likely to be comfortable with them second time around. Some aspects differ between girls and boys more now than before, so it may be that the first boy and the first girl experience more restrictions and tension then others in the family. On the other hand, each child is asserting his or her identity as clearly as possible in the early teens, so it is a grave mistake to think that they can be treated the same way as a brother or sister, anyway.

It is always worth bearing in mind family position, however, and the expectations that an older child's experience will have set up for their younger siblings. They need to be allowed the same privileges and opportunities at the same stage, as far as possible, in order for everyone to feel that they are being fairly treated. With some things, therefore, such as allowances, curfews and chores, we may need to negotiate and agree guidelines only once, and then use them consistently with each child.

READY TO GO: LEAVING HOME WITHOUT LEAVING THE FAMILY

If parents feel that the 'elastic' of parent–child bonds is being stretched in the first ten years of life, the next decade or so may feel more like bungee-jumping. We watched a number of volunteers hurl themselves from a bridge into an 80-metre gorge in the Pyrenees. Crowds had gathered at the roadside to watch, and it was spectacularly tense and thrilling. One man dived stylishly, head first into the abyss, almost as if he had wings rather than an elastic rope round his heels. We cheered and marvelled at his confidence and forgot our fear on his behalf. But the second, having prepared identically, donning harness and rope, seemed rather to tumble from the bridge's parapet, only to be thrown lurching from side to side across the ravine, his body at odds with the bouncing and jerking, looking insecure and awkward all the way. That was terrifying to watch, and a total contrast to the first bungee-jumper. Both men were perfectly safe, however, held by the strong elastic and the safety harness, and were eventually lowered to the bottom of the gorge, to walk back up a path and meet their friends and supporters.

Parenting in the later teens may feel as nerve-wracking as this: at times our children seem to bound forward effortlessly and stylishly, leaping confidently into new situations. They are hope-filled and free, off to college, off on holiday, driving themselves, adults at last. Their confidence, however, like the first bungee-jumper's, is in being securely attached: they may leave home for holidays, for college terms, or for good, but they never leave the family. At other times, they are more like the second bungee-jumper: there is a crisis, they seem to have no sense of purpose or direction, they 'fall into' jobs, relationships and decisions, and are uncomfortable with themselves, not knowing who they are or where they're going. Yet at these times the 'elastic' of family ties is equally crucial—to stay in touch and attached, to encourage and reassure, to love and to pray.

A long stretch…

Some children need to 'stretch the elastic' further than others: in several families, the 'middle' child seems to fall into this category. In establishing their own identity as adults, some will need to move away from the family, either geographically or in their outlook and values. This can, of course, be very painful for parents and for siblings too. It may be unresolved sibling rivalry that actually motivates the move. A younger sister reflected on the keen competition between her two older brothers. The older brother was sent to boarding school, then went to university and never felt a part of the family unit again. This left the younger brother, the middle child, feeling inadequate and a failure, despite being his parents' 'favourite'. He went abroad and finally emigrated, only visiting his home country twice in the next forty years. The breach at the point when he left, in his early 20s, was painful and 'put the lid on any close relationships we might have found', in his sister's words. Although his parents began to heal the breach with visits abroad, his father's early death arrested the process and left all the family with deep regrets still keen in the memory.

Another mother mused over her middle child, who has worked abroad for three years in his early 20s, but now chooses to return to live closer to parents and siblings, and seems more at ease with himself and his future plans than ever before. Interestingly, he has kept in closer contact with his siblings through this period than with his parents, by phone and e-mail, discussing problems and plans with his older brother in particular. The bond with parents was very strong before he left, and it has survived, largely because they have had the wisdom to allow the elastic to stretch, almost unbearably far at times.

Flying the nest

She suddenly realized that after Toby left to go travelling, he'd probably never live at home properly with the family again. For him, after the trip would be university, then work, and grown-up life. They'd finished being children together, now they'd have to work out a way of being separate adults.[4]

Children leaving home is the last 'key point' we will consider, and these thoughts of a younger sister encapsulate what this stage entails for sibling relationships.

Usually, however, the focus of attention is on the parents left behind—the 'empty nest' syndrome—which may have a traumatic effect on parents themselves and on their relationship. This is because it is a major change of role for parents, and in some cases a change of identity too, if their primary sense of who they are is focused on caring for the children. It is crucial to anticipate and prepare for this stage, especially when the last child in a family is about to leave home.

The effect on siblings at this point is equally dramatic. The dynamics of the family shift rapidly, especially if older children are away at college and home for holidays. The oldest child has the responsibility of being 'the first to go' in most, but not all, families. This will involve working out a new and more adult relationship with parents, and also keeping in touch with siblings and being a bridge for them between the two worlds of home and college, or family and work. Happy the family in which the older sibling tries to include their younger brother or sister in their 'new life' to some extent, by having them to visit or stay for a weekend, perhaps, or simply by keeping in touch via phone, letters or e-mails. Visits home will then be a lot less tense, and the older child will find adjustment to home much easier. Coming home can be very difficult, and good communication is essential, often facilitated by siblings when it is strained between parents and children. Parents do well to remember that the young person's priorities for their holiday will include catching up with friends from home, as well as, and perhaps more immediately than, time with their families.

For the younger siblings, especially those close in age, a whole new world opens up as they watch their older sibling fly the nest. A middle child may now find himself or herself the oldest in term time, but will then have to change role when the older sister or brother comes home. The situation of the youngest child in a family is particularly acute at this point. Having had one or more older siblings around all their life, they may now become an only child in term time, with the new privileges and pressures that this entails, especially in terms of how they relate to parents. They are then thrown back into being the younger brother or sister of the returning student(s), eager to do things with them during the holidays, and often resentful of time they spend with their friends or away from home. The church community can ease some of these tensions if students return to a youth group of which their younger siblings are now a part, so that they have friends in common and socialize together.

Away at school

All these adjustments apply equally if children are at boarding school, particularly if siblings remain at home when they go away. As this happens at an earlier age, when sibling bonds and the child's sense of their own identity are less well-formed, the effects are often long-lasting. Sadly, some adults would attribute tensions and breakdown in relationships to one child being 'sent away' from parents, especially when others were not.

'My parents left me in boarding school in the UK when I was nine and took my younger sisters abroad with them... I found this very difficult,' wrote someone in their 40s, who found it hard to build close relationships with siblings as a result.

Clearly, the ethos of boarding school has changed tremendously in the last thirty years, so that close contact with families is much more possible to maintain. It is important to consider the effect on every family member and on all the relationships in the family, however, not just on the child who is going away and the parents. Siblings who are close will miss each other tremendously. Parents need to recognize this and facilitate contact between them, without resenting it if this contact excludes them as parents. The bonds between siblings often provide the greatest incentive to 'come home' at this stage. Indeed, over the next few years, as the children in a family become young adults, the strength of their relationships with each other will often determine the health of the family and its closeness, every bit as much as the parent–child bonds do.

Position in family may become less significant, although one oldest child told me how her siblings still look to her for advice, even in their 30s. The sense of 'seniority' and responsibility remains strong for older siblings for many years. Peggy, a lifelong member of our church, was telling me about her sister coming to stay after a spell in hospital. I asked her if they were close in age, as well as in relationship. 'Oh no,' she replied. 'She's five years younger than me—she's only 90!'

High ideals

Psychologists list eight attributes of the analytic ideal of human maturity:

- to experience love more than hate
- to enjoy realistic pleasures and accept realistic frustrations
- to have a sense of identity
- to possess a role in the family
- to accept sexual wishes without guilt
- to acknowledge a wide range of emotions
- to be able to communicate with freedom
- to have an absence of neurotic symptoms such as phobias, compulsions or deep depression.[5]

Every one of these attributes has a relational emphasis and can be fostered within sibling bonds, peer relationships and close friendships. In this chapter we have been concerned especially with the third attribute—the sense of identity. Though shaped in the family, this sense is most often put to the test outside the home, at school, with friends, eventually in adult life. As teenagers assert their own identity, they are likely to seek either to be different from others, or to try very hard to be part of the crowd. As they negotiate their way between these two extremes, we hope that they will reach a sense of who they are—what they value, like, hope for, and dream of. Paradoxically, the more secure they become in their own identity, the more they are likely to be aware of others and of the community in which they live. Each person's experience of family life will continue to influence them long after they have ceased to live with their parents, and the effects of this can be seen most obviously if they go on to have children of their own. Those who have lived in a healthy family will have acquired many skills and perspectives which equip them for life as a whole, particularly in terms of how well they relate to other people.

❖

BIBLE FOCUS: SHOULDER TO SHOULDER MOSES, AARON AND MIRIAM

One of the greatest figures of the Old Testament, Moses, was threatened with death as soon as he was born. The Israelites in Egypt were becoming too numerous, and although the king needed a large workforce, he was anxious that they could pose a threat to his power, so he ordered all boy babies to be killed. Shiphrah and Puah, the Hebrew midwives, disobeyed this decree because they were faithful to God, and were rewarded by God for their courage with families of their own. Moses' life story begins with this marvellous illustration of individual faith, though it is interesting to note that Shiphrah and Puah acted together in their defiance: how much support and resolve they must have gained from each other as they stood shoulder to shoulder in front of Pharaoh (Exodus 1:12–22).

The threat is now broadened to be a national command that all Hebrew males should be thrown into the Nile at birth. Moses' parents, God-fearing members of the tribe of Levi, cannot bring themselves to destroy their beautiful son, and instead hide him for three months before placing him in a basket in the reeds at the edge of the river. This basket boat (the same word in Hebrew as the ark that saved Noah and his family) becomes the rescue vessel for God's chosen leader. The waters of destruction become the waters of life: Moses is found by a princess and his life is spared.

Big sister knows best

At this point, Miriam, Moses' elder sister, takes a risk herself. She is waiting nearby to see what will happen to her baby brother, and to report back to their anxious mother. When the princess finds the child, and while her natural compassion for the infant is still strong, Miriam acts fast. She offers to find him a Hebrew nurse, before the princess can pause to recognize the illegality of the situation. So Miriam nips home to her mother, who returns to the princess, is employed by her to look after the child, and goes home again with Moses in her arms. The baby she gave up to God's care has been restored to her. The brother whom Miriam thought she had lost has come home. Faith in God is rewarded, but in Miriam and her mother's case, just as for Shiphrah and Puah, it is decisive, active and risky. Moses spends the next few years of his childhood in his family, with Miriam and his brother Aaron, who was born three years earlier, presumably before Pharaoh's decree was made.

Remarkably, Moses' mother gives up her son a second time when she takes him back to Pharaoh's daughter, who adopts and names him. The princess gives Moses a Hebrew name meaning 'pull out', a constant reminder not only of his true identity as an Israelite, but of his escape from death and of his future role in leading Israel out of slavery. Moses grows up as a foreigner in the Egyptian court, gaining an education far beyond that available to his fellow Israelites, and being equipped for the task ahead. We might expect the story to be straightforward from here on, now that the difficulties surrounding Moses' birth have been negotiated. But Moses is far from ready yet to be the leader of God's people.

Angry young man

As we read the account of Moses going to watch the Israelite slaves working, and lashing out in anger at an Egyptian who is beating one of them, we see all the passion, impetuosity and fire of youth. Moses murders the foreman, hides the body and tries to get away with it. When, next day, he tries to intervene between two Hebrews who are fighting and to pronounce judgment on the aggressor, they turn on him: 'Who put you in charge of us and made you our judge? Are you planning to kill me, just as you killed that Egyptian?' (Exodus 2:14).

Reading this with hindsight, the man's comment is laden with irony: Moses will be put in charge of his people and made judge over them, but only in God's time, and when he is ready for the job. Moses is clearly a natural leader; he has also been brought up to fear God and identify with his people, so he assumes that he can take on the might of Egypt and change the world overnight. It is so easy to condemn his action, but it is born of righteous anger at the injustice and oppression that his own people are suffering. There is no doubt where Moses' loyalty lies. He may have been brought up in the Egyptian court and benefited from all the privileges of the ruling class, but he knows his roots—he has not forgotten who he is. Without this passionate commitment to Israel and to justice, he could never have become their leader and judge.

Exile experience

Moses is forced to flee, to leave both the pleasures of Egypt and the plight of his people. He must have headed for the desert weighed down with regrets; he must have thought he had blown it completely. The bigger the mistake, the more we learn from it, however, and Moses, if he is to be of any use to God, needs to learn that he can do nothing on his own. His own reactions have led to disaster; he needs humbly to learn to depend on God himself. The training ground for this is to be Midian, where the people are descendants of Abraham by his second wife Keturah, nomads who live in the desert as shepherds. It is a life that prepares Moses in many ways. He marries a Midianite, Zipporah, and has a family. He lives with his in-laws, including his wise father-in-law Jethro, who takes him into his home as an Egyptian refugee. Moses' experience of family life, of desert life and of exile in a foreign country during this forty-year period will prove invaluable in the forty years to come. His relationship with Jethro continues to be a source of support and good advice for many years (see Exodus 18).

Different doors

There is much to learn from this account of Moses' early adulthood. Our society expects young people to be in the driving seat, to be able to take on leadership and responsibility as soon as they have paper qualifications. The pressure to succeed, to make your mark and your first million by the age of 30, can be huge. This pressure can come from families as much as from those at work: we want our children to know where they're going and to get there as soon as possible. But in God's plan, the journey is every bit as important as the destination. Just as it took forty years for Moses to be ready to lead Israel, it took forty years for the people to be ready to enter the promised land. What might look like a waste of time—literally travelling round in circles in Israel's case—is the necessary process of learning to trust and obey God. What a different perspective this could bring to our parenting! It takes time to learn from experience, and mistakes are not so much dead ends as detours along the way, times of learning and growing.

We were discussing this one evening with friends, considering the decisions and choices that our children were beginning to make. We realized that each of us, at the end of our schooling, had made mistakes or had experiences that seemed disastrous at the time—a family bereavement, failure of exams, rejection by a university, and so on. Yet, looking back, we could all see God's hand on our lives at that time, and how the 'mistakes' had become opportunities for growth, learning and change, from which we had all benefited, not so much in the short term as in the directions our lives had taken as we looked back over twenty years. We resolved to be open to 'different doors' for our children, to hold on to a longer-term view for them. As our grandmothers would have said, 'When one door closes, another door opens.' I would rather be a person who holds that other door open than a person who stands by the first door condemning or despairing because things have not gone according to plan. It is only by taking risks and getting it wrong that we learn to take risks and get it right.

Consider this version of the story:

Moses had succeeded in freeing the children of Israel from their slavery in Egypt. It had been difficult, for the Pharaoh had been stubborn, and it was only after the death of the firstborn in each household that he finally agreed to let them leave.

Pharaoh had always been changeable—every time something had happened, he had promised to let them go, and every time things got better, he changed his mind. This time it was no different—each day as Moses led his people away from Egypt, they could see the cloud of dust raised by the pursuing soldiers loom larger as Pharaoh gradually caught up with them.

It was then that disaster struck. Stretching right across the horizon ahead Moses saw the Red Sea. There was no way round, and no way across, and Moses knew that Pharaoh's army would catch up with them the next day if they were to stop.

Moses told the people to camp at the side of the sea, and went away by himself in order to pray about it. After a night's prayer God told him what to do. He had to stand with his staff outstretched over the sea and the waters would part.

And so Moses and his people were marched back into captivity and slavery. But Moses comforted himself with the thought that he'd done his best; and he marched back into captivity knowing that he had not made a fool of himself by standing with outstretched arm over the sea.[6]

Sibling support

Once Moses is ready to take on God's mission, he is made aware of the task ahead in a dramatic fashion, encountering God in the burning bush. He puts forward all the objections he can think of to God's plan, but finally accepts his role and heads back to Egypt with his wife and children. He is unable to tell Jethro the real reason why he is returning—nor, perhaps, to explain it to Zipporah either, we are not told. What we do know is that, as he had promised, God sends Moses' brother Aaron to meet him and to go with him to Pharaoh. The reunion is recounted briefly: 'The Lord sent Aaron to meet

Moses in the desert. So Aaron met Moses at Mount Sinai and greeted him with a kiss' (Exodus 4:27).

Behind this episode lies a wealth of meaning—Aaron's obedience to God's command, the significance of meeting at the mountain which was to become the place of God's meeting with his people, and the love and loyalty denoted by the older brother's kiss. However rocky their relationship may have been during the years of Moses' exile, it is now restored. Sibling support gives Moses the courage and confidence to view new horizons, and to take risks of a magnitude he could never have foreseen, even in his fiery youth. Remarkably, he and Aaron are accepted immediately as the leaders of their people. I wonder if Aaron and Miriam paved the way for their little brother's return. From this point on, Aaron and Miriam are with Moses all the way and we are only told of two occasions when their support for each other breaks down. Perhaps these occasions stand out because they are exceptions, and because they are dealt with very severely in each case (see the fourth 'Growth point' below). Thus Moses' very identity as a leader is defined in the context of his relationship with his siblings—Aaron the priestly leader, and Miriam the prophet and leader of all the women of Israel.

❖

IN A NUTSHELL

In this chapter we have considered the importance of communication with teenagers, in the family and in other stable relationships outside the home. We looked at the need to encourage responsibility and independence, even when it means allowing young people to make mistakes. The key stage of young people leaving home raises issues for parents and siblings.

Finally, the analytic ideal of human maturity was outlined and discussed briefly. (See the third 'Growth point' below.)

The story of Moses' early life provided examples of (a) a wrong action that led to learning, and (b) the importance of the family base and sibling relationships in Moses' discovery of his true identity.

GROWTH POINTS

- 'The aim is to affirm, not to threaten; to care, not to criticize' (see page 127). Can you think of situations in which you have received such affirmation and care? When have you been able to give these qualities to someone else? Are there relationships in your life at present where these qualities are needed?

- Think of any young people you know in your family or church who are about to leave home or have recently done so. What are their needs, and those of their family? How could these be met?

- Look again at the ideal of human maturity on page 134. Think further about any aspects that ring true in your own experience.

- For further Bible study, read Exodus 32 and Numbers 12:1–16. What do these stories tell us about the relationships between Moses, Aaron and Miriam? Look at Moses' reaction in each case: what can we learn from this? What light does this shed on God's view of how siblings should relate?

CLEARINGS

RISKS

*To laugh is to risk appearing
the fool
To weep is to risk being
called sentimental
To reach out to another is to
risk involvement*

To expose feelings is to risk
showing your true self
To place your ideas and your dreams before the crowd
is to risk being called naive
To love is to risk not being
loved in return
To live is to risk dying
To hope is to risk despair
To try is to risk failure
But risks must be taken because
the greatest risk in life is to risk nothing
The person who risks nothing
does nothing
has nothing
is nothing and
becomes nothing
They may avoid suffering and sorrow
but they simply cannot learn, feel, change, grow or love
Chained by their certitude, they are a slave
They have forfeited their freedom
Only the person who risks is truly free.[7]

PRAYER

A CELTIC BLESSING FOR THOSE WHOM WE LOVE

May God be with thee in every pass
Jesus be with thee on every knoll,
Spirit be with thee by water's roll,
On headland, on ridge, and on grass

Each sea and land, each moor and each mead,
Each eve's lying-down, each rising's morn,
In the wave-trough, or on the foam-crest borne,
Each step which thy journey doth lead.[8]

NOTES

1 Robert Shure, *The Ring of Words*, ed. Roger McGough, Faber and Faber, 1998, p. 10
2 Bowlby, *A Secure Base*, p. 2
3. *Raising Cain*, p. 163
4 Judy Astley, *Muddy Waters*, Black Swan, 1997
5. *Raising Cain*, p. 164
6 Kairos Group, *Jesus is Alive*, Falcon, 1972, p. 99
7 Attributed to Janet Rand, source unknown
8 George McLean, from *Praying with Celtic Christians*, SPCK, 1988, p. 39

CHAPTER 8

SIBLINGS MATTER: THE CHALLENGE TO THE CHURCH TO BE COMMUNITY; GROWING THROUGH MUTUAL DEPENDENCE AND TRUST

> *The idea of family has been used, not just as a description of how people actually live, but also as a metaphor for how people wished their lives had been. The idea of a family has a powerful grip on people's imaginations and represents something over and above their actual experience. The family is invested with significance because it expresses, perhaps more vividly than any other idea, a sense of collective well-being.*[1]

THE WAY WE LIVE NOW

Try asking your friends and relatives what a family is. The answers are likely to range from memories of childhood to sitcoms with 2.4 children, or maybe an impossible dream or an outdated institution. The word 'family' means very different things to each person, depending on their own experience; but nonetheless, for better or worse, families matter.

Before the last General Election, the British Prime Minister broke with tradition by announcing the date in a school rather than outside Number 10 Downing Street. His message was clear: we are looking to the future, to our children and young people—they are our priority. As always, political parties vied with each other to occupy the moral high ground. The surest route to the summit was to endorse 'family values', to be seen to be the party that most effectively supported family life and invested in children's futures, whether by raising spending on education or introducing 'baby bonds'. There is no doubt that 'the family' remains high on the political agenda but, with rising divorce rates, the birth rate now at only 1.64 per mother, and ever-increasing financial and work pressures on parents, isn't the institution as we know it in grave danger of extinction?

We have considered many aspects of family life in these pages, some of them usually overlooked in contemporary society. I believe passionately that the family can be the greatest source of happiness, security and fulfilment. Equally, and paradoxically, it can be the opposite, robbing its members of all of these blessings. All who care for children, whether in families, schools or churches, need to be alert to pressures that threaten to undermine family life. Consumerism is one such pressure.

Born to shop?

In some quarters, and certainly in the commercial world, children are now viewed as being acceptable only if they are cute mini-adults, sharing adult interests and values. Jackie Cray, speaking about passing on values to the next generation, gave a fascinating analysis of contemporary family life. She talked about the BBC TV children's series, *Tellytubbies*, and the uproar it initially provoked. One journalist described the programme as 'slow, silly, banal and incoherent', with 'characters who are repetitive and don't talk properly'. As Jackie pointed out, it is not just *Tellytubbies*, but babies, who are banal, repetitive and don't talk properly, and the whole furore surrounding *Tellytubbies* was a sad comment on our so-called sophisticated society, which can't tolerate babyish behaviour. In fact, the very word 'babyish' is now often used as an insult.

At the same period as *Tellytubbies*, there was a TV advertisement featuring a baby in a supermarket trolley who spoke in an adult voice, commenting wittily on his parents' behaviour; and films with similar themes, such as *Look Who's Talking*. Commercial interests now seek to mould our children into consumers from infancy, with the attendant financial pressure that this places on the whole family.

Can't buy me love

Thus, as our material standard of living and expectations have risen, the family has fallen victim to consumerism. Our consumer age is turning babies into another desirable commodity, and then turning children into consumers as soon as possible. Advertisers raise the stakes in parent–child relationships by putting pressure on parents to provide the newest and best of everything for their child. The media portray the perfect family, eating a perfect family meal in a spotless and tidy designer home, full of shiny appliances and trendy furnishings. Every year, 80,000 advertisements on television are aimed at children, who then put pressure on their parents to buy them 'must have' goods. Yet in Sweden, advertisements aimed at under-12s are banned. In a TV documentary, a spokesman explained, 'We want our children to have their childhood, not to build up consumerism.'[2] The vital relationships upon which each person's future well-being depend risk being devalued into little more than commercial transactions, or scarcely valued at all. Parents under pressure are likely to put pressure in turn on their children to achieve and produce, when childhood is really about being and becoming. We are, after all, human beings, not human doings. Almost thirty years ago, the psychologist John Bowlby pointed out that our society's values were dangerous: 'Man and woman power devoted to the production of material goods counts as a plus in all our economic indices. Man and woman power devoted to the production of happy, healthy and self-reliant children in their own homes does not count at all. We have created a topsy-turvy world.'[3]

Royal remembrance

When the Queen Mother died in March 2002, many people felt that it was the end of an era, and were deeply affected by the event. At the Queen Mother's funeral, the Archbishop of Canterbury reflected that it was the sense of family, rather than the public royal role, that had evoked such warmth in the British people towards the 'Queen Mum': 'She personified family values, the hopes and dreams, and rose-tinted memories of community during the Blitz.'

The funeral, followed a few months later by the celebrations of the Queen's Golden Jubilee, gave rise to many 'rose-tinted memories' in the media. Had life really changed so much in a century, or in fifty years? And was it change for better or for worse?

Raw edges

What clearly have changed, in the royal family and in society as a whole, are the patterns and structures of family life. The results are often confusing and disorientating, especially for older people, and those living on the margins:

On the outer estates, there is very little sense of community, but many older people reminisce about the sense of togetherness engendered within the older, often condemned housing from which they were rehoused... 'We were always popping in and out of each other's houses, and didn't even have to lock our doors'... One has the clear understanding... of a people facing the present and the future together... It is equally clear, at this raw edge of our postmodern generation, that the family structure, so beloved in those past days, has lost its power. The conventional lifestyle of a married couple and children is extremely weak on the estates. As a result, traditional moral and spiritual values are becoming ever more and more flimsy.[4]

This is more widespread than an individual, family or church concern. In contemporary society, the sense of community, and of individual identity within that community, is being eroded by our fast-changing lifestyle. There are a number of reasons for this, one of which is suggested by John Benton: 'As society has grown numerically, and as it has become increasingly urbanized with people living in vast towns and cities, life has become increasingly anonymous. The village community, where everyone knew and accepted one another, is gone. People do not get the recognition they used to have.'[5]

As an adopted Londoner, I take issue with such a bleak view of city life, for it is possible to find a sense of community in an urban setting, provided that people can establish roots and build relationships. The dangerous sense of 'anonymity' is, however, familiar to many. Two current trends identified by estate agents and sociologists suggest ways in which people are trying to rediscover their identity within a community.

Granny hopping

The first trend is for grandparents to move considerable distances in order to live close to their children and grandchildren. One in five sets of grandparents interviewed for a radio feature gave 'living close to grandchildren' as their top priority when choosing where to live. One grandfather expressed his feeling that their children had missed out through the death of their grandparents when they were very young, and that he wanted to get to know his grandchildren as they were growing up. A grandmother talked of wanting to be available to babysit or help when people were ill, and specifically of releasing the young parents to take time out on their own: 'If I can give that to strengthen their marriage and family life, I'd like to do it.' The other benefit of this move was seen to be the proximity of the family as the grandparents got older, when they might need help in return.

Back shifting

'Back shifting' is the second trend, in which the move to the affluent south is being reversed, as many people choose to return home to the places in which they grew up. A radio discussion of the phenomenon featured a television producer who had left London for his native Liverpool and spoke of the strength he drew from the familiarity of his own background and culture. Others valued the support network of 'people who know who you are', and expressed the importance of being 'rooted', in a period when life is full of risks and holds little job security. Fifty percent of the population, we were told, live within half an hour of their parents, and forty percent of married people still regard their parents' house as 'home'. The sense of where we come from, the discussion concluded, is vital to our sense of who we are. The enormous popularity of 'Friends Reunited' and similar internet sites also proves the hunger many people feel to reconnect with and belong to a community.

CHALLENGE FOR THE LOCAL CHURCH

Rather than bemoaning social disintegration, I believe it is vital for the local church to be active in unconditionally supporting *all* families and providing a safe place where people can find acceptance, friendship and healing. This is far from the image of the church that many people hold, feeling judged and condemned for not living up to particular standards.

Which of us has not experienced the pain caused by broken relationships in our families? Often, when families meet for a wedding, funeral or christening, there are differences and hurts simmering under the surface. When these events take place in a church building, the church can provide a safe environment for meetings and steps towards reconciliation to begin. It is part of the church's calling to pray for and encourage such family restoration.

A single mother bravely attended an evening to discuss the significance of having her baby christened, with other parents and the minister of her local church. At the end of the meeting she expressed her relief that she was included and accepted. She had come along because she had attended the church primary school and felt that she still 'belonged' in some way to the church, although she had not attended for years. It was the start of a renewed relationship with that young woman and her family, but it could so easily have been the end of any contact with her, if the church had been too quick to judge her situation.

Support for families is also part of equipping and training those who can build community in future, and the local church is uniquely positioned to model a positive, proactive and Christian attitude to marriage and parenting. Community-based projects such as parenting courses, drop-ins, toddler groups, after-school care and holiday clubs all meet real needs and make a real difference to families. They also help to send out a message to those around, that Christianity is about love rather than judgment, and compassion rather than criticism.

Expand and include

Make a conscious effort to achieve a sense of belonging for every family member, adult or child, step or biological, custodial or non-custodial. Expand your definition of a family to include stepparents, stepchildren, custodial and non-custodial children.[6]

This advice to stepparents is good advice for all families, and for churches too. As we have seen, accepting and including people is vital if they are to feel they belong, either in a family or a church community. They can then give and receive love and support. A church member commented on the difference her 'home group' has made:

We have almost no family in the UK and they have been family to us. We have known that we and our children are welcome in their home and their lives. Knowing that they have been praying for us all has been a wonderful blessing, as are the lasting friendships we have formed in the group.[7]

Christian organizations also seek to provide this acceptance in the camps and holidays they run for children and young people:

Good at sports or bad, clever or hopeless, they find in camp an inclusive and accepting spirit which sets them free to be themselves... It's the combination of teaching with developing relationships in a genuine Christian community which makes the camp method so effective.

And it all works best when the special experience during the holidays is part of a regular, weekly experience in a local church or SU group.[8]

Horizontal health

'Family' is so often considered only in terms of parent–child relationships, both in the 'designer baby' boom and, sadly, in the custody battles and access arrangements with which many parents now have to grapple in order to see their children. 'Horizontal relationships', whether between siblings or partners, are then put under great strain, and this can jeopardize the stability of the whole family. Thus, in 'blended' families, the danger is that the parent–child bonds take priority over the new marriage or other adult partnership: 'Family relationships are likely to be disturbed if the primary coalition is between two generations.'[9]

We urgently need to recognize the importance of horizontal relationships, not only between partners, but between siblings, cousins, stepsiblings and friends, to redress the balance and stabilize the 'family tree'. This father, speaking to his teenage daughter, saw exactly how crucial her relationship with her brother was to the whole family:

I don't expect you to be perfect. I get angry at times too. But I do expect you to share my love, and your mother's love, with your brother. You cannot demand exclusive rights to it. We are a family. We should be able to live together in harmony, helping each other, not tearing each other down.[10]

Jesus recognized the importance of 'horizontal' relationships when he taught his disciples about the church using the image of a vine, where horizontal, as much as vertical, growth is vital.

Growing together

Stay joined to me, and I will stay joined to you. Just as a branch cannot produce fruit unless it stays joined to the vine, you cannot produce fruit unless you stay joined to me. I am the vine, and you are the branches. If you stay joined to me, and I stay joined to you, then you will produce lots of fruit. But you cannot do anything without me... You did not choose me. I chose you and sent you out to produce fruit, the kind of fruit that will last. Then my Father will give you whatever you ask for in my name. So I command you to love each other.

JOHN 15:4–5, 16–17

The vineyards of southern France are a wonderful sight in summer. Place names straight from wine labels mark the route through the villages. Vines hang heavy with dark, dusky branches as the grapes ripen and mature. No wonder the wine tastes so full, rich and sun-drenched. But it is hard work to produce such a harvest. The vines are tended with care and precision. Rows range in age and maturity from the spindly young stems of new plants to the lush green screens of foliage in which one plant is indistinguishable from another. New plants are constantly being grafted on to the rootstock to provide an unbroken supply of healthy, fruit-bearing plants. At this early stage, the graft is protected—'bandaged' until it has taken properly and become fully assimilated into the vine. The young plants need plenty of support: each has its own stake and the wires along the rows provide a further support as the branches reach upward and outward. As the individual plants age, they grow together until the whole row appears and grows as a single vine, each part of it leaning on and supporting the others. Where one plant fails, a young one will be added into the space, and nurtured between two older, stronger plants until it is integrated into the whole.

Principles for people

Two important principles for families and churches emerge from the vineyard.

First of all, integration is vital. Note that new plants are not grown from packets of grape pips, but from a graft from the rootstock, which means that every plant is part of the same 'true vine'. For wine producers, this gives a consistency to the grapes grown—their flavour and other characteristics—and the wine produced will retain its distinctive quality. In families and churches, there will be a sense of belonging—being part of the same wider community—and with this, a commitment to each other in mutually supportive relationships, as the example earlier from a home group member demonstrated.

Second, new life is carefully protected and nurtured. We are used to this in the family setting, in which babies and young children need careful and consistent protection in order to thrive. In the church setting, care of babies and children is equally vital, and needs to be of high quality. Yet so often, the crèche is in a dark corner or an outer annexe. What message does that give about the importance of nurturing young lives in the church?

In addition, those who are young in faith, or new to the church, need to be receivers of care rather than being pounced on to help with coffee, flowers or Sunday school the minute they walk through the door. It takes time for people to feel at ease in a church community, to get used to how things are done and who is who, and to make friends. Only once this graft has taken will their faith grow stronger; only then will they be in a position to give as well as to receive. It is a key part of the minister's role, within the relationship which she or he has with the church member, to sense when this point is reached, and to suggest appropriate ways of involvement in the church community. This will often need considerable patience and faith, to wait for the right time rather than being driven by an urgent need. If the new plant is expected to produce fruit before the graft has taken, or to grow strong without adequate support as it begins to push out new branches, it is unlikely to survive (see the third 'Growth point' on page 163).

We have thought about the importance of 'horizontal' relationships in the family and the local church. We have considered the pressures on family life in contemporary society. We have looked at lessons from the vineyard about nurturing and supporting one another. Before drawing to a close, however, please join me for a brief and not altogether irrelevant digression.

Literary detour

The car slowed as it turned off the main road and I woke up. As is my wont on a hot afternoon, I was dozing, while Nick drove us home from the New Forest, and I had hoped to stay asleep for most of the trip back into London. This detour was unexpected, but a very pleasant surprise as we stopped at Chawton, former home of Jane Austen and now a museum in her memory. I read her novels while still at school, I dissected them as a student, and I have since enjoyed them over and over again on page and screen. Jane Austen was a parson's daughter, the seventh of eight children. Two of her brothers found fame and success in their naval careers, and lived far more exotic and privileged lives than Jane. All were wealthier. She never married, had children or travelled widely. Yet her writing has more than withstood the test of time. Why?

Jane Austen writes about human relationships, primarily those of family and friends, which were the ones she herself experienced. She was very close to her six brothers, and especially to her sister Cassandra, whose children she also adored. At various stages after her father's death, she lived with her brothers in Southampton, Bath and finally Chawton. Her sister accompanied her to Winchester to stay near her doctor during her final illness, and Jane died in her arms. We know so much about her life because she was a prolific letter writer, corresponding regularly with her siblings and friends. The nuclear and wider family networks were her life, and her art. The characters in Jane Austen's novels have a universal appeal, despite their lifestyle, which is centuries removed from ours. Readers or viewers today can still identify with their feelings, motives and dilemmas, and she makes a convincing case for the importance of strong sibling relationships by showing those that work and those that don't. Thus, at the end of *Sense and Sensibility*, the story that has enjoyed renewed popularity since the major film adaptation in the late 1990s, we read: '... and among the merits and happiness of Elinor and Marianne, let it not be ranked as the least considerable, that though sisters, and living almost within sight of each other, they could live without disagreement between themselves, or producing coolness between their husbands.'[11]

Sibling sense

To have a close relationship with your siblings, then, is a thing to be worked for and highly prized. I believe that this is why Jane Austen is still so popular, when the formal, 'good-mannered' relationships between men and women that she describes are now alien to our culture. The characters who can really talk to and confide in each other are siblings and friends, and these are not 'second best' to the marriage partnerships and parent–child relationships: they are the source of much mutual support, contentment and love.

Shakespeare too values positive sibling relationships very highly. Perhaps this is because life expectancy in Elizabethan England was much lower than it is today, and because women were so dependent on their male relatives for all material sustenance. The reunion of siblings Sebastian and Viola at the end of *Twelfth Night* is every bit as moving and significant as the resolution of their romantic entanglements. Filial affection is a strong force, often seen to be more enduring than sexual love. Sibling divisions, on the other hand, lie at the heart of Shakespeare's most powerful tragedy, *King Lear*. The lack of love shown by Lear's daughters, both for their father and for each other, is heartbreaking because it seems so unnatural and amoral, yet it echoes in family experience down the centuries.

It is interesting to note how TV serials depend on the tangled relationships of families, often large and complex ones, for their drama. The Slater family in *EastEnders*, for example, provides endless storylines as the five sisters love and hate, rescue and betray each other. Were they not sisters, and, in one case, a mother and daughter who have grown up as sisters, we would not really care. But blood is thicker than water in Albert Square, and probably everywhere else too. Family relationships exert an immense power in our lives, such that this comment from a psychologist could be a trailer for a soap opera: 'The home is the setting in which the most ardent ties of love are formed and the deepest hatreds simmer.'[12]

Friends for life

The fact was that we had known each other all our lives but we had never gotten tired of each other.[13]

For many today, it is sibling relationships that can offer continuity and support when their parents' relationship breaks down, or when they are faced with the challenges of life with stepparents and in stepfamilies. When sibling bonds are strong, they are a source of support and security.

'She's my life-raft' was the succinct description given by one woman of her sister, even though they now live on opposite sides of the Atlantic ocean. 'We get on very well—better than ever... He is still protective and I look out for him too,' wrote a man of his older brother. Another adult told me how her younger sister had confided in her first, before talking to her parents about her unplanned pregnancy. Siblings can offer each other empathy and acceptance throughout their lives, even when they are not particularly close. Often, it is only in later life that bonds are reinforced: 'Dad had various disagreements with his siblings, which resulted in long silences! As he grew older he realized the need to keep the family together and he grew closer to siblings and more reliant on their support and love.'

The death of a parent is a time at which siblings especially benefit from the mutual support they can give and receive. One of the most poignant aspects of the Queen Mother's death was the Queen's isolation, even in the midst of her large family, because of the death of her sister, Princess Margaret, just six weeks earlier. By contrast, the solidarity of the grandchildren who walked behind the coffin exemplified the support of siblings and cousins in their loss.

One woman, whose sister died a few years before her mother, wrote movingly of her loneliness: 'It would have been good if she had survived Mum, so as to be there for each other at that time.'

Another wrote this about her brother: 'We don't see each other very often and I suppose as adults we have very different views on life. We don't keep in touch that well either. When we do get together it is very comfortable and I feel that there is still a strong bond between us.'

Relational skills

The principle of being 'very comfortable' with someone who may now be very different from us is extremely important. We learn so much about relationships in our families, both positive and, sadly, negative. Those who have related positively to siblings, parents and an extended network of relatives and friends will have both the ability and desire to do so in the wider community. 'The family is where we learn our relationship skills. And the way we relate to our children and teach them to relate to each other, even in the heat of battle, can be our permanent gift to them.'[14]

These skills can, and should, also be modelled and learned in the local church. The actress Jane Horrocks is aware of this as she describes the 'horizontal' as well as 'vertical' dynamic of church:

I have always believed in God and was taken to Sunday school as a child— and I want to do the same with my children. I love the community aspect of churchgoing; for example, it's the only time I have any contact with the elderly. I see going to church as a way of connecting with a life beyond my own—and I quite often come away with the answers.[15]

It is crucial in our contemporary society, when many have given up on 'family' as a flawed and outmoded institution, that the church takes seriously its call to be a body, a group of people who relate to each other and live lives which are interdependent, not isolated. For 'family' remains God's plan for human life—not in a narrow, restricting sense, but in the broadest and deepest sense of creating strong, loving relationships between people, who may or may not be linked by blood.

⁜

BIBLE FOCUS: A BETTER WAY

As Jesus was walking along the shore of Lake Galilee, he saw Simon and his brother Andrew. They were fishermen and were casting their nets into the lake. Jesus said to them, 'Come with me! I will teach you how bring in people instead of fish.' At once the two brothers dropped their nets and went with him.

Jesus walked on and saw James and John, the sons of Zebedee. They were in a boat, mending their nets. At once Jesus asked them to come with him. They left their father in the boat with the hired workers and went with him.

MARK 1:16–20

I wonder if you have ever thought about how many of Jesus' very first disciples were siblings. In fact, six of the twelve joined with a brother, and the family bonds must have been fundamental in beginning to knit the group together. In John's Gospel, Andrew hears Jesus' call first and goes to fetch his brother Simon, who returns to Jesus with him. This scene was beautifully portrayed in the recent film animation of Jesus' life, *The Miracle Maker*, where the closeness and trust between Andrew and Simon Peter is very clear. In Luke's Gospel, we are told that Simon, James and John are partners, so presumably the brothers knew each other already and were used to working together, although, as Jesus told them, they would be involved in a very different kind of work from then on. It is also interesting that these three form the central core of Jesus' 'team' in the later stages of his work, and become the key leaders of the early Church. Strong relationships bear much fruit.

Team talk

Many managers of sports teams have followed Jesus' example. All the world's most popular male team sports have been enriched by brothers playing together, most famously (in England), Jackie and Bobby Charlton in the 1966 England World Cup winning soccer team. The world of motor racing has been fascinated by the rivalry between brothers Michael and Ralph Schumacher, who race against each other in a very dangerous sport, with no love lost between them on the track. This would be hard to bear were it not for the sense of fraternity between all the drivers, who pit their skills not just against each other but against the track, the machine and the weather, and who will often be the first at the scene of an accident trying to rescue their 'brother' driver.

Currently, sisters Venus and Serena Williams dominate women's tennis, but have often failed to produce their best play when competing against each other.

In fact the sisters could not find it in themselves to challenge and compete with one another. That was more than a shame, for it robbed the public and robbed themselves. Since only the sisters can extend each other at present, only they can force each other towards their potential.[16]

Venus and Serena far prefer to play with each other. This is how Serena describes their doubles partnership: 'We just laugh and giggle. It's just a more relaxing environment because you're out there with your best friend. You're able to relax and it helps us play better.'[17]

Team building

So Jesus built his team around brothers, and two pairs in particular. When we look through the Gospels for evidence of how this team building progressed, we see the disciples at their most human and can identify with their doubts and arguments, 2000 years later. Most famously, James and John ask to be given priority over the others, and Jesus restates the fundamental truth, 'If you want the place of honour, you must become a slave and serve others!' (Mark 9:35).

In Matthew's account of the incident, James and John's case is pleaded by their mother, to the extreme annoyance of the other ten disciples. Jesus reminds them all, 'If you want to be great, you must be the servant of all the others. And if you want to be first, you must be the slave of the rest. The Son of Man did not come to be a slave master, but a slave who will give his life to rescue many people' (Matthew 20:26–28).

Co-operate or compete?

Any close relationship can end in rivalry if we allow it to. Recent television game shows have played on this very conflict between co-operation and competition. Friends are invited to put their relationship under pressure by competing against each other; partners and siblings are invited to test their loyalty to breaking point; and competitors in the *Big Brother* house are invited to denigrate their fellow housemates in order to have them evicted and save their own skins. Competition makes good entertainment, but we also know that, in real life, it can cause immense damage to both winners and losers, if there is not sufficient support and affirmation in the rest of their lives.

Jonny Wilkinson became the hero of the media and the nation as he helped England to glory in the 2003 Rugby World Cup, yet he consistently affirmed the importance of the team as his reason for playing well. Even in the dizzy heights of victory, the team was paramount to him:

I can't describe the feeling. Not just winning the World Cup but being part of a team and feeling that togetherness... We've taken our fair share of hits from everyone. But we've believed in ourselves and we've always stuck together.[18]

Mend it like Beckham

Teamwork matters to losers as much as to winners. In the 2002 Soccer World Cup, England lost to Brazil, the first goal coming as a result of an error by the goalkeeper, David Seaman. Newspapers blamed him, recalled all his past mistakes and made him a national scapegoat. The team, however, was far stronger than that. A photograph of Seaman being hugged by his captain, David Beckham, appeared on the front of a Christian newspaper a few days later, with these words:

Some people are on the pitch. They know it's all over. David Seaman is inconsolable. If only. If only... Beckham, the so-called villain of England's previous World Cup campaign, clutches his keeper. He knows the feeling. Along with millions of other England-shirt wearers, he wishes it hadn't happened. Surely Beckham understands how hard it is to forgive yourself. He knows what it is like to take the blame. Knows what it is to be accepted back again. That's why he can side with Seaman. He knows he is his keeper's brother.[19]

Co-operation is not usually fashionable in the media, but then good news rarely is. How relevant and challenging Jesus' words are! Over and over, he drives home the lesson, to his disciples and to us—co-operation, not competition.

It is the same lesson that Joseph and his brothers had to learn, and which faced the father Jacob just as dramatically as a younger man. Miriam and Aaron were punished harshly for trying to compete by undermining Moses' leadership. The elder brother of the prodigal son probably missed the party because he was too self-centred to rejoice at his brother's return. Only by overcoming the tyranny of self, which is part of our human make-up, can we become the people God wants us to be, in relationship with others.

This remains Jesus' challenge to us all, in our families, our churches and communities: 'You must love each other, just as I have loved you. If you love each other, everyone will know that you are my disciples' (John 13:34–35).

❖

IN A NUTSHELL

The final chapter has reviewed the state of 'the family' today, and how it has changed. The dangers of anonymity and consumerism pose threats to family life.

The challenge to the local church is to offer support to families, through groups which nurture and model healthy relationships, drawing on the biblical image of the vine.

Sibling relationships, present in well-known literature, are as relevant today as ever, and can be a source of support and friendship throughout life.

The 'Bible focus' section looked at Jesus' choice of disciples, highlighting both the strengths and the pitfalls of sibling relationships, summarized in the principle of co-operation, not competition.

GROWTH POINTS

- Is our view of family in the past too rosy? What could help us to look forward with confidence rather than backward with regret?

- 'The family has fallen victim to consumerism.' What evidence of this have you seen in your own or other families? Think of ways to combat materialism in your own situation.

- In what ways have you experienced integration, protection and nurture, (a) in your family, and (b) in your church? Are you in a position to offer these qualities to others? How?

- For further Bible study, read Matthew 20:20–28 and Luke 22:24–27. From Jesus' teaching to his disciples, discuss what it means in practice to be servants, (a) in our families, and (b) in the church. How can we promote and encourage this servant attitude?

CLEARINGS

THE NEW COMMANDMENT

My dear friends, I am not writing to give you a new commandment. It is the same one that you were first given, and it is the message you heard. But it really is a new commandment, and you know its true meaning, just as Christ does. You can see the darkness fading away and the true light already shining.

If we claim to be in the light and hate someone, we are still in the dark. But if we love others, we are in the light, and we don't cause problems for them...

From the beginning you were told that we must love each other. Don't be like Cain, who belonged to the devil and murdered his own brother... If you hate each other, you are murderers, and we know that murderers do not have eternal life. We know what love is because Jesus gave his life for us. That's why we must give our lives for each other.

1 JOHN 2:7–10; 3:11–12, 15–16

PRAYER

Lord, make me an instrument of thy peace.
Where there is hatred, let me sow love.
Where there is injury, pardon.

Where there is discord, vision.
Where there is doubt, faith.
Where there is despair, hope.
Where there is darkness, light.
Where there is sadness, joy.

O divine Master,
Grant that I may not so much seek to be consoled as to console;
To be understood as to understand;
To be loved, as to love;
For it is in giving that we receive,
It is in pardoning that we are pardoned,
And it is in dying that we are born to eternal life.[20]

NOTES

1. *Something to Celebrate: Valuing Families in Church and Society*, NS/CHP, 1995, p. 18
2. *Hard Cash*, BBC TV, 14 May 2001
3. Bowlby, *A Secure Base*, p. 2
4. Wallace and Mary Brown, *Angels on the Walls*, Kingsway, 2000, p. 183
5. John Benton, *Christians in a Consumer Society*, Christian Focus, 1999, p. 164
6. *Stepfamily Problems*, p. 110
7. From *Platform One*, magazine of St Stephen's church, East Twickenham, July 2002
8. *@SU*, Scripture Union Scotland, June 2002
9. *Stepfamily Problems*, p. 135
10. *Raising Cain*, p. 6
11. Jane Austen, *Sense and Sensibility* (first published 1811), Penguin edn., p. 322
12. *Raising Cain*, p. 1
13. Jane Smiley, *A Thousand Acres*, Flamingo, 1992, p. 62
14. *Siblings without Rivalry*, p. 240
15. Quoted in a commemorative brochure for the centenary of Kensington Episcopal area, 2001
16. *Sunday Times*, 7 July 2002
17. *Sunday Times*, 6 July 2002
18. *Sunday Times*, 23 November 2003
19. *Christian Herald*, 6 July 2002
20. Anonymous, c. 1913, *A Time to Pray*, Lion, 1997, p. 200

EPILOGUE

RETURN TO THE PARK

Autumn once again; not floods this year but high winds, which felled a number of trees in the park, trees still heavy with October leaves. I walked down to the river past the black walnut and felt a physical shock at the sight of two massive limbs lying on the ground. The devastation was still stark and disturbing, several weeks after the storm. A helpful notice from English Heritage explained that the debris would be cleared away as soon as possible, and the fallen wood used in a sculpture project as part of celebrations for the centenary of the park's opening to the public, the following year. It also outlined the conclusions reached by tree experts after a comprehensive inspection:

- The first large limb to fail had extensive heartwood decay.
- The second limb failure occurred at a point where an old pruning wound was present. This wound allowed drying of the heartwood and subsequent lack of flexibility.
- The trunk and main branch structure are sound with no evidence of decay or structural weakness.

So what of the tree? Lopsided now, and crestfallen, its generous embrace has been curtailed and the scars of missing branches are raw and pale against the black bark. The black walnut tree was tested by the storm and suffered in it, but it's still standing and growing, however altered and imperfect. The trunk is as broad and solid as ever, supplying nutrients to its lateral boughs, and the horizontal branches that remain are clearly healthy, their 'heartwood' supple enough to withstand the gale.

It doesn't take an expert to understand that it's the heartwood which is crucial. If this dries out and eventually decays, through blockages in the internal structure, the whole branch is at risk. The parallels with human relationships and the need for good communication are clear. Our 'horizontal' relationships will also survive and be sources of support within the family only if they stay flexible, kept healthy by taking time, offering encouragement, and demonstrating unconditional love. A parent of teenage boys, whose own relationship with a sibling helped them through their parents' divorce, commented:

We always tell them, 'Be good to your brother. He is the one person who will always love and support you', and they do genuinely seem to have a close loving relationship (although neither would admit it, of course!). I spend a lot of time balancing my time between both boys so neither feels less valued. They do compete for our attention and approval and we often remind them that they are equally treasured.

Another parent, of younger children, expressed her pleasure at watching her children's relationship grow:

It has added an extra dimension to our family and it has been one which I have been able to enjoy and observe from the sidelines. I'm conscious that I have some influence on it but also there is a degree of my being independent of it. It's exciting to see it unfold.

A grandmother had similar thoughts: 'I don't really think that as parents we (or anyone) sets out with a policy. I think it's more your inbuilt values that come through, and lives unfold.'

The second branch to fall from the black walnut was lost at a point where an old pruning wound was present. These comments are typical of many families still living with painful memories: 'My mother was the eldest of three children. Her sister emigrated to Australia. Her brother had a disagreement shortly after my grandfather died, and they were never reconciled thereafter...'; 'My father hasn't seen his brother for about forty years after a family split and never talks about him...'.

Old wounds run deep, in families as much as in trees, and can be healed only through determined acts of acceptance and forgiveness, which enable us to let go of the past and its hold over our present lives. A woman wrote of her brother, now living in Canada, that he 'has hurt the family and now removed himself from us', but she added a postscript to her comments, that he had just sent her a card, with a letter, on her fiftieth birthday, in response to her daughters' optimistic invitation to the surprise party they had organized. This gesture she welcomed warmly, although it was not an easy decision to do so: 'He obviously wants to mend fences, which we will start to do.'

Circumstances will continually test the inner strength of our family relationships, and it may be the storms to which we look back as the times of most growth. The novelist Sue Townsend, reflecting on her struggle to bring up three children as a lone parent, comments: 'I don't just see good times or bad times: during the bad times, and out of them, wonderful things happen that leave you open to new experiences.[1]

Finally, a comment from a woman who grew up in a family of five adopted children, each with special physical needs. She explains that this made them all feel deeply loved as they were 'chosen', and that they are certainly as close as any 'blood tie' family. This family has faced many hard times, including the death of a parent when the youngest child was a baby, but it continues to be one which is growing strong:

I now get on very well with my two sisters. We have been through some extremely difficult and traumatic times but have weathered the storms. Now we are closer than ever, because we have complete trust.

NOTES

1 Sue Townsend, 'Best of Times, Worst of Times', *Sunday Times Magazine*, 15 December 2002

FURTHER READING

Barnes, Rob, *Winning the Heart of Your Stepchild*, Zondervan, 1997
Bridge, Sheila, *The Art of Imperfect Parenting*, Hodder, 1995
Britey, Anne & Mungean, Tim, *The Parentalk Guide to the First Six Weeks*, Hodder, 2001
Campbell, Ross, *How to really Love your Teenager*, Paternoster, 1999
Chalke, Steve, *How to Succeed as a Parent*, Hodder, 1997
Coates, Anne, *Your Only Child*, Bloomsbury, 1996
Collins, Gary, *I Believe in the Family*, Hodder, 1996
Dallow, Gill, *Touching the Future*, BRF, 2002
Dobson, James, *How to Build Confidence in Your Child*, Hodder, 2000
Faber, Adele & Mazlish, Elaine, *Siblings without Rivalry*, Avon Books, 1998
Fixter, Janice, *The Parentalk Guide to Being a Mum*, Hodder, 2000
Fowler, Deborah, *Loving Other People's Children*, Hodder, 1995
Frank, Penny & Stroud, Marion, *The Questions Children Ask/The Journey Parents Make*, CPAS, 1994
Frydenger, Tom & Adrienne, *Stepfamily Problems*, Spire, 1997
Harding, Jim, *The Parentalk Guide to Being a Grandparent*, Hodder, 2002
Henshaw, Steve & Ann, *Is This a Daddy Sunday?* Monarch, 1994
Jakes, T.D., *Help! I'm Raising My Children Alone*, Creation House, 1995
Meadows, Peter, *The Parentalk Guide to Being a Dad*, Hodder, 1999
Nouwen, Henri, *The Return of the Prodigal Son*, DLT, 1994
Omartian, Stormie, *The Power of a Praying Parent*, Kingsway, 1996
Parsons, Rob, *The Sixty Minute Father*, Hodder, 1995
Parsons, Rob, *The Sixty Minute Mother*, Hodder, 2000
Pearlman, Eileen & Ganon, Jill, *Raising Twins*, Harper Collins, 2000
Scott Evans, Paul, *Preparing to Parent Teenagers*, Paternoster, 1999
Spungin, Pat & Richardson, Victoria, *The Parentalk Guide to Brothers and Sisters*, Hodder, 2002

Strean, Herbert & Freeman, Lucy, *Raising Cain*, Facts on File, 1998
Watkins, Eleanor, *Survival Handbook for Freaked Out Parents*, Kevin Mayhew, 2000
Watkins, Eleanor, *Survival Handbook for First Time Parents*, Kevin Mayhew, 2001
Wigley, Judith, *Under Fives and Their Families*, Marshall Pickering, 1990

BOOKS FOR CHILDREN

PICTURE BOOKS

Andrae, Giles & Cabban,Vanessa, *There's a House Inside My Mummy*, Orchard, 2001
Anholt, Catherine & Laurence, *Sophie and the New Baby*, Orchard, 1997
Boon, Debbie, *Aunt Sal*, Macdonald, 1998
Carlstrom, Nancy White, *Before You Were Born*, Eerdmans, 2002
Godfrey, Jan, *Sam's New Baby*, Scripture Union, 1998
Hughes, Shirley, *Alfie Gets In First*, Red Fox, 1997
Hughes, Shirley, *Dogger*, Red Fox, 1993
Hughes, Shirley, *Wheels*, Walker, 1992
Hutchins, Pat, *Titch*, Red Fox, 1997
Levy, Janice,*Totally Uncool*, Lerner, 1999
Masurel, Claire, *Two Homes* , Walker, 2001
McBratney, Sam, *I'm Sorry*, Collins, 2000
McKee, David, *Not Now Bernard*, Red Fox, 1990
Moon, Nicola, *Something Special*, Orchard, 1995
Ross, Tony, *I Want a Sister*, Collins, 2001
Shavick, Andrea, *The Truth about Families*, Oxford, 2001
Waddell, Martin, *Grandma's Bill*, Macdonald, 1990

EARLY READERS

Garland, Sarah, *Shimmy with my Granny* (Family Poems), Macdonald, 1999
Hoffman, Mary, *Starring Grace*, Frances Lincoln, 2000
Hughes, Shirley, *Chips and Jessie*, Red Fox, 1996
King-Smith, Dick, *Sophie Hits Six*, Walker, 1992
King-Smith, Dick, *Funny Frank*, Doubleday, 2001
Lavelle, Sheila, *My Best Fiend*, Collins, 1988
McDonald, Alan, *Mark's Dream Team*, Oxford, 2002

Mooney, Bel, *I Wish*, Methuen, 1995
Mooney, Bel, *I'm Bored*, Methuen, 1997
Simon, Francesca, *Horrid Henry*, Dolphin, 2000
Wilson, Jacqueline, *Lizzie Zipmouth*, Corgi, 2000

OLDER READERS

Bawden, Nina, *Carrie's War*, Puffin, 1974
Fine, Anne, *Goggle Eyes*, Puffin, 1990
Fine, Anne, *Flour Babies*, Puffin, 1994
Fine, Anne, *The Granny Project*, Egmont, 2002
Garnett, Eve, *The Family from One End Street*, Puffin, 1978
King-Smith, Dick, *Noah's Brother*, Puffin, 1988
Lewis, C.S., *The Lion, the Witch and the Wardrobe*, HarperCollins, 1950
Morpurgo, Michael, *Dear Olly*, Collins, 2000
Nesbit, E., *The Railway Children*, Puffin, 1994 (first published 1906)
Pielichaty, Helena, *Simone's Website*, Oxford, 2002
St John, Patricia, *The Tanglewoods' Secret*, Scripture Union, 1997
Serraillier, Ian, *The Silver Sword*, Puffin, 1993 (first published 1956)
Streatfeild, Noel, *Ballet Shoes*, Puffin, 1994 (first published 1936)
Streatfeild, Noel, *The Growing Summer*, Collins, 2000 (first published 1966)
Wilson, Jacqueline, *The Suitcase Kid*, Corgi, 1993
Wilson, Jacqueline, *Double Act*, Corgi, 1996
Wilson, Jacqueline, *The Illustrated Mum*, Corgi, 2000

SUBJECT INDEX

Aaron 136, 140–1, 162
Abel 76–7
Abraham (Abram)..............33, 39–41, 43, 137
Adam 22–3, 26, 76–7
apologies 66–9, 74
arguments 68–9, 71, 76
attachment 104–18, 125
Austen, Jane 46, 154–5
availability 52–3
babies 29–39
belonging 121, 149–50, 153
blame 21, 23–4, 65–7, 69, 71, 160–1
brothers 38, 51, 57–62, 76–80, 97–101, 119–21, 130–1, 139–40, 158–9
building 15–8
Cain 76–7
childcare 47, 88
Church 13, 18, 35–8, 153–5
commitment 15–23, 32, 120, 137, 153
communication 14, 56, 74–5, 114–5, 126–7, 132
comparisons 55–6, 92–3, 99–101
competition 51, 99, 112, 130, 160–1
consumerism 146
co-operation 15, 160–1
cousins 57, 88, 115, 151
covenant 41, 119–22
David 24–5, 118–22
decisions 15, 86, 112, 127, 138
EastEnders 155–6
Elizabeth 23–4, 41–2
encouragement 31, 66, 91–4
Esau 78–81
Eve 22–3, 76–7
fairness 71
faith (see trust)
family breakdown 8–9, 19–20
family tree 9, 12, 24
fathers 37–8
first-time parents 29–34
forgiveness....................................61, 68–9, 81, 167

foundations..15–17, 25, 31
fratricide 76
friends 36–7, 67–8, 72, 115–7, 121–2, 154–5
gender 50–1
grandparents 117, 148
gratitude 38–9
guilt 22, 76–7, 108
habits 17–18, 86
holidays 88–9, 132, 150–1
home 25–6, 93, 100–1, 116–7, 128, 130–2, 149, 156
home groups..150
honesty 25, 68–9, 73–5, 91, 120
identity 105–6, 113, 115, 128–31, 134, 140, 148
individuality..50, 53
independence 73, 104, 107–9, 114–5, 117–8, 128
integration 152–3
Israel 80, 119–21, 136–40
Jacob 57–62, 78–81, 161
Jesus 16–7, 20, 24–5, 35–6, 59, 67, 97–8, 151, 158–61
John (the Baptist) 42–3
Joseph (Old Testament) 57–62, 161
Joseph (New Testament) 24–6
key points..................................32, 107–11, 131
leaving home 107, 129–31
letting go 104, 108–10, 114, 117
listening 34–5, 74–5, 114–5, 126
local church 9, 20, 34–6, 38, 149–51, 157
lone parents 111, 167
love 9, 12–3, 21, 41, 49, 69, 108, 127, 150–2, 155–6, 161
(see also unconditional love)
loyalty..15, 17, 20, 32, 120–1, 137, 160
marriage 12–3, 19–20, 150
marriage service 18–9
Mary..23–5, 42
maturity 69, 71, 75, 127, 134

media ... 19, 39, 66, 111, 146–7
memories ... 54, 61, 86–90, 117–8, 147, 166
Miriam ... 135–6, 140, 161
Moses ... 135–40, 161
mothers ... 34–7, 47–8, 104–5, 109–10
one-to-one time ... 51–5, 74, 109
only children ... 111–2, 132
parents ... 13–4, 29–36, 38, 47–8, 52–3, 56, 67–9, 74, 85–8, 105–12, 126–9, 131–4, 146
parenting courses ... 36, 65, 75, 106
play ... 72, 87–90
position in family ... 110–1, 129, 133
praise ... 91–2
prayer ... 34, 52, 85, 126
pregnancy ... 30, 32, 35
remembering ... 114–6, 126
repetition ... 89, 109
responsibility ... 24, 33, 54, 58–9, 61, 69, 73, 128, 138
risks ... 15, 70, 135–6, 138, 140–2
royal family ... 121, 147
'safe places' ... 117–8, 125, 149
Sarah (Sarai) ... 40–1
school ... 20, 66, 87–8, 91, 93, 114–5, 133
second children ... 47–8, 50
servant(s) ... 160
Shakespeare ... 155
sibling rivalry ... 65–6, 71, 73–7, 130
sisters ... 38, 51, 55–6, 75, 155–7, 159
personal space ... 53–5
stepfamilies ... 88, 150–1, 154
supporting families ... 14, 21, 34–8, 105, 145, 149–50
'taking the bait' ... 65–6
teamwork ... 159–61
teenagers ... 86, 106, 125–8, 134
time ... 17–8, 85–90, 101
toddlers ... 108–12
toddler groups ... 109, 150
touch ... 94
trust ... 15–17, 22–3, 75, 120, 126
twins ... 112–3

unconditional love ... 85, 94–7, 99–101, 117, 166
young families ... 35
youth groups ... 132
Zechariah ... 41–3

BIBLE INDEX

The Contemporary English Version (CEV) has been used throughout.

Genesis 2:15—3:24	22
Genesis 2:24	14
Genesis 4:1–16	76
Genesis 4:6–7, 9, 25–26	77
Genesis 25:19–34	78
Genesis 12:1–3	40
Genesis 16:7–14	40
Genesis 17:1–2	40
Genesis 17:19, 21	41
Genesis 27:1–45	78
Genesis 28:13–15	80
Genesis 32:9–12	79
Genesis 32:28	80
Genesis 35:27–29	81
Genesis 37:2	58
Genesis 37:26–27	59
Genesis 37:30	59
Genesis 39:21, 23	60
Genesis 41:38	60
Genesis 42:11, 13, 21	61
Genesis 43:14	61
Genesis 44:18–34	61
Genesis 45	63
Exodus 1:12–22	135
Exodus 2:14	136
Exodus 4:27	140
Exodus 18	137
1 Samuel 17:26, 28, 32	119
1 Samuel 17:58	121
1 Samuel 18—24	121
1 Samuel 20:42	121
Psalm 16:5, 10	120
Psalm 22:6	122
Psalm 25:14	120
Psalm 36:5–6	122
Psalm 55:12–14	122
Psalm 70:5	120
Jeremiah 17:7–8	7
Matthew 1:24–25	24
Matthew 7:24–27	27
Matthew 20:26–28	160
Matthew 23:28	67
Mark 1:16–20	158
Mark 9:35	160
Mark 10:14–16	36
Luke 1:5–25	41
Luke 1:13	42
Luke 1:38	23
Luke 1:43, 45	24
Luke 1:76–79	43
Luke 2:52	25
Luke 6:46–49	16
Luke 15:11–32	98
Luke 15:24, 31, 32	101
John 13:34–35	161
John 15:4–5, 16–17	152
Romans 7:18–19	49
Hebrews 11:1	15
1 John 2:7–10	163
1 John 3:11–12, 15–16	163

New Daylight, BRF's popular series of Bible reading notes, is ideal for those looking for a fresh, devotional approach to reading and understanding the Bible. Each issue covers four months of daily Bible reading and reflection with each day offering a Bible passage (text included), helpful comment and a prayer or thought for the day ahead.

New Daylight is written by a gifted team of contributors including Adrian Plass, Margaret Cundiff, David Winter, Gordon Giles, Rachel Boulding, Peter Graves, Helen Julian CSF, David Spriggs, Margaret Silf, Jenny Robertson and Veronica Zundel.

New Daylight is also available in large print and on cassette for the visually impaired.

NEW DAYLIGHT SUBSCRIPTIONS

❏ I would like to give a gift subscription
(please complete both name and address sections below)
❏ I would like to take out a subscription myself
(complete name and address details only once)

This completed coupon should be sent with appropriate payment to BRF. Alternatively, please write to us quoting your name, address, the subscription you would like for either yourself or a friend (with their name and address), the start date and credit card number, expiry date and signature if paying by credit card.

Gift subscription name _____

Gift subscription address _____

_____ Postcode _____

Please send to the above, beginning with the next January/May/September issue: (delete as applicable)

(please tick box)	UK	SURFACE	AIR MAIL
NEW DAYLIGHT	❏ £11.10	❏ £12.45	❏ £14.70
NEW DAYLIGHT 3-year sub	❏ £27.45		

Please complete the payment details below and send your coupon, with appropriate payment to: **BRF, First Floor, Elsfield Hall, 15–17 Elsfield Way, Oxford OX2 8FG**

Your name _____

Your address _____

_____ Postcode _____

Total enclosed £ _____ (cheques should be made payable to 'BRF')

Payment by cheque ❏ postal order ❏ Visa ❏ Mastercard ❏ Switch ❏

Card number: ☐☐☐☐ ☐☐☐☐ ☐☐☐☐ ☐☐☐☐ ☐☐☐☐

Expiry date of card: ☐☐☐☐   Issue number (Switch): ☐☐☐☐

Signature (essential if paying by credit/Switch card) _____

❏ Please do not send me further information about BRF publicaations.

NB: BRF notes are also available from your local Christian bookshop.   **BRF is a Registered Charity**

www.brf.org.uk

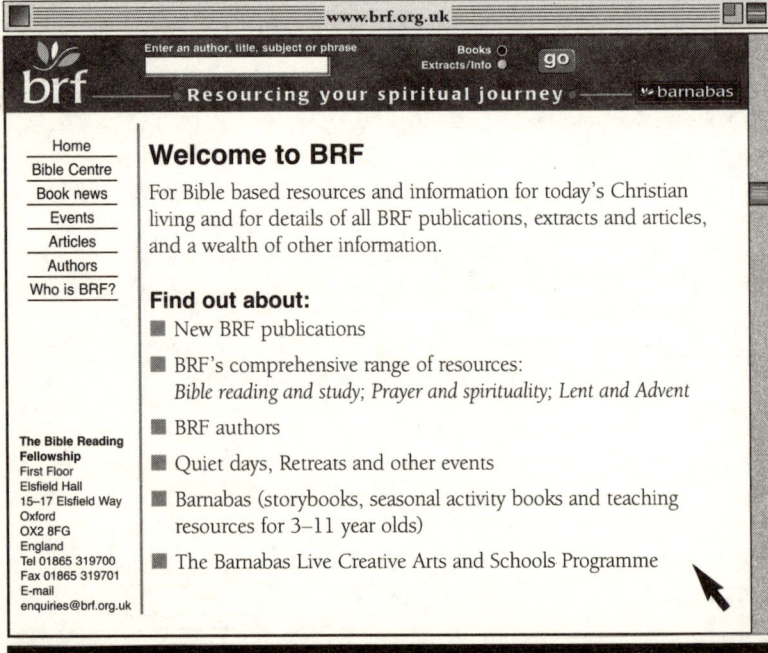

Enter an author, title, subject or phrase • Books ○ Extracts/Info ● **go**

brf — Resourcing your spiritual journey — barnabas

- Home
- Bible Centre
- Book news
- Events
- Articles
- Authors
- Who is BRF?

The Bible Reading Fellowship
First Floor
Elsfield Hall
15–17 Elsfield Way
Oxford
OX2 8FG
England
Tel 01865 319700
Fax 01865 319701
E-mail
enquiries@brf.org.uk

Welcome to BRF

For Bible based resources and information for today's Christian living and for details of all BRF publications, extracts and articles, and a wealth of other information.

Find out about:
- New BRF publications
- BRF's comprehensive range of resources:
  Bible reading and study; Prayer and spirituality; Lent and Advent
- BRF authors
- Quiet days, Retreats and other events
- Barnabas (storybooks, seasonal activity books and teaching resources for 3–11 year olds)
- The Barnabas Live Creative Arts and Schools Programme

Visit the BRF website at www.brf.org.uk

BRF is a Registered Charity